acting religious

acting religious

THEATRE AS PEDAGOGY IN RELIGIOUS STUDIES

victoria rue

The Pilgrim Press
Cleveland

To

DOROTHEE SOELLE

muse and revolutionary mystic

To my parents,

CATHERINE AND JAMES

whose creativity gave me life

The Pilgrim Press, 700 Prospect Avenue, Cleveland, Ohio, 44115-1100
thepilgrimpress.com

Printed in the United States of America on acid-free paper

09 08 07 06 05 5 4 3 2 1

Library of Congress Cataloging-in-Publication Data

Rue, Victoria, 1946–
Acting religious : theatre as pedagogy in religious studies / Victoria Rue.
p. cm.
Includes bibliographical references.
ISBN 0-8298-1629-1 (pbk. : alk. paper)
1. Drama in religious education. I. Title.

BL42.R84 2005
203'.7—dc22

2005051246

contents

acknowledgments

IT WAS NOT UNTIL I WAS SELECTED to be a member of the American Academy of Religion (AAR) Western Region Lilly/Luce Teaching Workshop 2000–2001: Teaching in the Global Village: Teaching Religious Studies and Theology that I understood that my years of using theatre techniques and plays in religious studies classrooms might be of interest to others. I offer my deepest gratitude to the members of that group who appreciated and encouraged my work: Heather Ann Ackley Bean, Laura Ammon, Linda Barnes, Kathlyn A. Breazeale, Pamela K. Brubaker, Grace G. Burford, Rudy V. Busto, Linell Cady, Kimberly Rae Connor, Marilyn Gottschall, Fran Grace, Amir Hussain, Zayn Kassam, Luis Leon, Lara Medina, Bruce M. Sullivan, Karen Jo Torjesen, Jeffrey VanderWilt, Randi Jones Walker, and Glenn Yocum.

During the writing of this book I shared chapters with my colleagues David Copelin, Kimberly Rae Connor, and Kelley Raab. David's dramaturgy and playwriting eye helped me clarify my theatre applications to religion. From the very beginning, as part of the Lilly Group, Kim Connor offered affirmation and support to my work. With humor, grace, and insight, she gave me suggestions that always made my work more understandable on the page. Kelley Raab, a colleague with me at St. Lawrence University in the Religious Studies department, keenly looked over several drafts of these chapters. Thank you!

Thank you to Mary Hunt for believing in my work and taking me by the hand to meet Pamela Johnson, my first editor at The Pilgrim Press. My gratitude to Pamela for her consistent support for the idea of this book.

Ulrike Guthrie, who inherited me from Pamela, has made this entire process of publication enjoyable. Thank you for your thorough and clarifying editorial comments that always inspired my work to be better.

Thank you to my dear sister, Monica Rue McQueen, for making this book a "sister act!" with your imaginative drawings, used by permission in chapters 2 and 3.

Thank you to my father, James Rue, for your encouragement of my work.

For the presence of your continual love and support these fifteen years, Kathryn, I am always grateful.

introduction

My passion is embodied learning. Through thirty years as a theatre director, playwright, and teacher, I've learned that students engage best with material when their bodies are active participants in the learning process. I have found this to be particularly true in teaching religious studies and theology. When the arts become part of the education journey, students learn on both cognitive and experiential levels. Pedagogically, the arts are not only tools for communicating in the global arena; they are also models for cooperation, community building, and somatic learning. With this approach, when I teach theatre-related courses, I bring my training in social justice and theology, a perspective that makes theatre an ethical and social enterprise. In religious studies programs, on the other hand, I use a blend of teaching modes that include seminar-style student learning and dramatic enactment. So for example, in courses I have taught such as introduction to religious studies, western religious traditions, biblical drama, mysticism, feminist theologies, and millennial thinking I have used theatre as an embodied technique for learning.

I am concerned about how religion is being taught in high schools, colleges, and congregations. Given the urgency and extremity of today's world events, it seems all the more pressing that we seek new approaches and new understandings of religions and religious experience to impart to our students. How are we to think otherwise when the newspaper reports that high school students in Pennsylvania taunted and hit a young Muslim girl saying, "Kill the Muslim; go home!" Where are the roots of this violence lodged? In dualisms of good and evil? In the families of the taunting children? In their schools that may have courses in ethics or world religions? As a teacher I must look at how my teaching—particularly my teaching of religion—shapes my community. New ideas and new approaches must awaken our understanding, empathy, and compassion.

But courses in religion need more than a cognitive understanding of central concepts. Students need to viscerally encounter belief, religious practice, religious imagination, and religious experience. Religions are more than ideas: they are lived, enacted by human beings in particular ways.

This book offers teachers at the college and high school levels as well as religious educators within congregations a resource for embodied learning through theatre.

MY RESEARCH, INSIGHTS, AND EXPERIENCE

In the seventies, my work in the theatre as a director and playwright was part of a larger movement, that of feminist theatre. Feminism in the seventies was excavating women's history. So much of it had been misplaced and edited out. Women's literature was being rediscovered. As a playwright, I found that I was drawn most to women's novels, poetry, and short stories rather than plays. That choice made me "think outside the box" to invent "seeable" theatrical expressions of complex literary ideas and forms. I created plays from the poetry of Sylvia Plath, the novels of Collete, Isabel Allende, and Susan Miller, the letters of Natalia Danisi Murray and Janet Flanner, as well as short stories by Katherine Mansfield and Joyce Carol Oates.

In tandem with this work, I began teaching what poet and playwright Honor Moore and I called, "Women Writing-Women Telling." These workshops guided participants to excavate their own experience as the resource for their writing. Honor devised writing exercises and I created theatre exercises that stimulated memory and inspired women to give words to their experiences. The writers then wrote for thirty minutes. Afterwards, each piece was explored dramatically through silent gesture, movement, and eventually words. Different narratives called for different explorations. A poem in a single voice might become a Greek chorus, a story that used narrative and dialogue was acted out with characters speaking in both the first and third persons. Sometimes a free improvisation on the idea of a written piece was used to stimulate the writer into revisions of her work.

This playful theatre work served to expand each writer's initial draft in both content and form. When a writer saw her work embodied, she saw it anew. When a writer heard and saw her written work enacted through the bodies of other participants, she felt her words. She felt the experience that was held inside the words. Likewise, audiences at the plays I created with Plath's poetry met the searing electricity of her words through the actors' bodies, voices, gesture, and movement. Plath's experiences were unlocked and shared. When joined with actions, words crackle with meaning, are heard in new ways, enter into us to stay. This is essentially the experience of theatre.

In both theatre performances and the Women Writing-Women Telling workshops, unleashing the power held inside words/narratives/poetry was also an act witnessed by a group of people. For a moment in time, each enactment created a shared experience among those who watched. This sharing forms the seeds for building community. Classrooms can be arenas for building communities too.

When classrooms become communities of learning, students and teachers are "rehearsing" the society they would like to see.

In the eighties, I began teaching theatre as a playwright and director. For me, acting classes were a laboratory, a place to further explore what it meant to create feminist theatre. Work with student actors meant helping them reinhabit their bodies—since negating the knowledge of the body is a legacy from western civilization and Christianity. Learning to inhabit the whole body, students engaged in body, movement, gesture, and voice exercises. Improvisations were occasions for affirmation. Students shared their life experiences and their peers witnessed them. In scene analysis, student actors discovered relationships between their own lives and a character in a play script. They learned the give and take of dialogue with other characters, entering into relationship with the other. Experiencing acting classes and engaging in the process of making theatre also introduced students to teamwork and the pleasures and responsibilities of being part of an ensemble. This is the experience of community building. Overall, my approach to teaching acting was an act of empowerment, for my students, and for me. With the conclusion of each course, we all stepped into our "gotta make it" world with a clearer sense of ourselves and our connectedness to one another. For me, these are crucial components of feminist theatre.

The mid-eighties found me going deeper into myself and my work as an artist. I continued teaching and directing, but I found my inner resources needed water.

I'd gone to Nicaragua for a conference with other theatre artists and saw there, for the first time, base communities (communidades de base). These church communities worked to create clean water and street lights as acts of prayer. They used theatre to teach children health and safety as well as liberating interpretations of biblical stories. Here, I witnessed for the first time progressive Christianity creating social transformation with the poor. I returned to New York City inspired. Perhaps by coincidence, I met a new Master of Divinity graduate (M.Diva is more fun, don't you think?) of Union Theological

Seminary (NYC) who was going on to study neurology in medical school. She said in her work with the pandemic of AIDS, she knew she needed a spiritual base. I understood then that Union was the place. There I could water my inner resources and refresh my commitment to social change.

At Union, at the age of thirty-eight, I became a student again in the classrooms of Beverly Harrison, Dorothee Soelle, Janet Walton, Phyllis Trible, and James Cone. Feminist, womanist, and liberation theologies seeded my renewed Christianity and future pedagogy. In the chapel services I often helped to create, we witnessed the combustion of ritual and theatre. I realized how feminist theatre can enact feminist theology. It was too inspiring to stop learning! I continued into doctoral work in "theology and the arts" at the Graduate Theological Union in Berkeley. During all the course work and dissertating both at Union and the GTU, I found myself constantly "pushing the envelope" with my professors. I had learned well from the feminist movement that my experience as a woman and theatre artist was important, so of course I wanted to incorporate my considerable theatre experience into my studies! My research papers became plays, my sermons became dialogues, my liturgies became dramatic enactments. What I knew was theatre. Through it, ideas could be enfleshed. This was the genesis for my dissertation, "Feminist Theatre Enacts Feminist Theology in the Play 'CancerBodies: Women Speaking the Unspeakable.'"[1]

During and following my Ph.D., I taught in both seminaries and colleges and drew upon theatre to embody ideas. All the acting exercises I had previously generated to help students express themselves and engage with play texts now found a home in my religious studies classroom. All the chapel services of Union became visceral memories that guided me in teaching embodiment to theology students. It was clear: theatre offered encounter and the opportunity to inhabit the ideas of the classroom.

This book is a compilation of exercises that I used in those courses. Chapter 1 maps the intersections of theatre and religion and makes the case for embodied teaching and learning. In the chapters that follow, I offer specific theatre exercises for energizing and focusing your classroom. I suggest simple theatre techniques to awaken the body, voice, and mind. Other theatre exercises describe how to build trust and community while allowing students to see that the body (without words) can communicate. Chapter 3 instructs how to open the discussion of a classroom topic using theatre exercises such as thematic sculptures. Chapter 4 suggests how to use improvisation in the classroom. Improvisation is understood as a method to deepen the classroom's discussion of a topic. The chapter also explores the creation of characters, situations, and scenes to embody and explore authors and ideas. Chapter 5 demonstrates how to use writing, memorization, and performance to deepen students' experience of sacred texts. Chapter 6 guides teachers in using dramatic plays in the classroom. Dramatic plays offer rich resources for embodying religious ideas and principles. Chapter 7 illustrates ways to evaluate the creative work of students when theatre is used in the religious studies or theology classroom. Chapter 8 explains the comfort/fear spectrum for teachers who are breaking new ground in their pedagogy by using theatre in the classroom. The conclusion offers a summary and reiterates a call for embodied pedagogy in the religious studies classroom.

Students are eager to experience something new. Clearly you are too if you are reading this book. Theatre in your religious studies classroom will change you and your students and their experience of learning.

1

why theatre as a pedagogy?

Instruction cannot begin with God
but must connect to people's experience.
And one of the central experiences is that
the self's seclusion is broken open.

— DOROTHEE SOELLE
The Silent Cry

IT'S THE FIRST DAY OF CLASS. The course is Introduction to Religious Studies. The course description has alerted students to the use of theatre. "Take off your shoes, please; you are on holy ground—the holy ground of creativity! Put your books and papers aside, push back the desks, and form a circle." This is the place from which we begin. These three actions—taking off shoes, pushing back desks with books, and creating a circle—contain the key elements of our explorations into religion and theatre: the body, relationship, everyday experience, and community. At the same time, the request signals a new pedagogical method, perhaps even a new way of knowing.

Drama and religion are old acquaintances, having known long periods of both friendship and estrangement. Drama emerged from the church to the church square, from the temple into the marketplace. The history of drama is a history of secularization.[1] Yet one underlying principle of drama has always been the discovery of one's self in the story of another. This truism is also theatre's link with religion. The knowledge of our connectedness to one another through empathy with another's feelings is simultaneously the experience of theatre and the experience of love and forgiveness.

Yet, "acting religious" seems to point to artificiality—superficial piety—actions without meaning. With the title of this book, my intention is to evoke the image of artificiality in order to ask, what is religious experience? How does intentional action intensify bodied experience? "Acting religious" also seems to suggest that acting is deceiving, lying. Not so. Acting is about entering into another's experience with your own experience and realizing something new from the combustion that occurs. *Acting Religious* is at once a call to experience meaning and a theatre method to embody it.

The religious studies introductory course I often teach is entitled "Mystery and Meaning." My intent is to explore to what extent students can enter into the mystery and meaning held within religions through empathy and somatic experience. Whether it is meditation or poetic mysticism or how a religion is lived in everyday life, the journey is an embodied search for meaning that leads us ultimately to unknowing, to the ineffable, to mystery. In the classroom, the search is not undertaken alone; in fact, in recognizing our interdependence we enflesh mystery, not for answers, but for the wisdom that comes from community.

Theatre is the campfire around which we share the stories of the community. Theatre embodies our struggles and delights. Theatre's stories enact mystery and meaning. Actors offer lived experience to an audience and are witnessed and affirmed by them. The audience empathizes and reimagines their own journeys anew. Theatre is an enfleshment, an incarnation, a groping, stumbling attempt to approach and understand our world and beyond our world. As plays help us to reimagine those worlds, so the process of making theatre is a laboratory for testing those visions. Theatre as a laboratory is a space to enact human experiences of love, forgiveness, anger, peace. In this way, theatre becomes a rehearsal for what we would like to see happen in our lives. Theatre can also be a laboratory for religion, where ideas and visions can be experienced.

Because I am a theatre artist as well as a religious studies professor, teaching works best for me when it is an experience of the mind and body. Discovering feminist theology in the 1980s while at Union Theological Seminary, I was inspired by its commitment to the primacy of women's bodily experiences. It is through this lens that I connect my theatre-making to teaching religion. By the late eighties I understood that the principles of feminist theatre—body, relationship, experience, and community—were the same principles found in most feminist approaches to religion.

THE BODY

Theatre is all about the body. When we watch a play we are witnessing bodies moving in space and time. If we are part of an improvisation or scene, we must use our bodies to communicate our character's predicament. Bodies communicate through gesture, mobility/immobility, rhythms, and sound.

Religions have historically seen the body as "the other" and in need of control. A feminist approach to religion understands our bodies as the site of the Holy. Honoring and caring for our own and each other's bodies is an experience of the Divine. It was particularly my study of Christian mysticism that led me to understanding the necessity of the body. The women mystics of the Middle Ages speak of God as a sensory experience. "Let Him kiss me with the kiss of His mouth!" says Teresa of Avila.[2] Mechthild of Magdeburg expresses the anguish of desire when she says "God burning with His desire looks upon the soul as a stream in which to cool His ardor."[3] Mysticism is not a mental encounter with the Divine. It is a full body experience.

Feminist ethicist Beverly Harrison further situates the body:

> Women do not merely have bodies. The body-self is the integrated locus of our being in the world. . . . The experience of beginning to live from the center of ourselves outward has invigorated women with a new sense of spiritual power. . . . Such a spirituality takes seriously the full range of conditions necessary for human well-being in the world.[4]

In describing the relationship of embodiment to women's sense of participation in the world, Harrison is challenging religions to think, feel, and act. This "integrated locus" is what poet Audre Lorde called our "lifeforce." Studying religion out of this integration requires teacher and students to do the same. The use of theatre in teaching offers a method for this integration. Theatre is thinking, feeling, and acting—with the body.

The body is the text upon which everyday experience is written. Bodies are living texts in their brokenness and joy.

> Women's bodies are the most sensitive receivers for historical reality. Their bodies record what has happened in their lives. Their bodies remember what it is like to be no-body and what it is like to be a some-body.[5]

The text of the body contains the history of women and men's wellness and illness. To read the body of one's own text can be an act of courage. To read each others' texts is to meet and be permeated by another's lived stories. For example, think of Helen Keller's startling experience of discovering the association between a word and its "body."

> As the cool stream gushed over my hand my teacher spelled into the other (hand) the word "water," first slowly, then rapidly . . . suddenly I felt a misty consciousness as of something forgotten—a thrill of returning thought; and somehow the mystery of language was revealed to me. I knew then that w-a-t-e-r

> meant the wonderful cool something that was flowing over my hand. The living word awakened my soul, gave it life, hope, joy, set it free. . . . I left the well-house eager to learn. Everything had a name, and each name gave birth to a new thought.[6]

The action of the water poured over the hand, its coolness and fluidity against the skin, awakened an inscribed memory held within Helen Keller's body. When we realize that our bodies contain the knowledge of experience, we touch the living word that is life. In appreciating our bodies as troubling and exuberant texts, the incarnation of women's and men's bodies is revealed. Body as living sacrality is revealed. When we hear another's story and know it lives in and through that particular body, we awaken to the other's life and come into relationship.

As students recognize that our bodies are texts, we act differently toward ourselves and one another. To live with our bodies as texts means to honor the histories that are imbedded there. To live with our bodies as texts means we must honor all texts, in all shapes and colors. To live with our bodies as texts, we do not privilege the interpreter, but rather the subject. Our bodies record what has happened to us in our lives. Each of us viscerally sustains and re-members joy and suffering. Each carries his inscribed stories. Students and teachers' bodied experiences are living connective tissue in learning with the heart and head.

The traditional notion of a teacher—immobilized behind a desk or lectern—symbolizes an immobile body of knowledge.[7] When a teacher moves out from behind the lectern to use theatre techniques, for example, her actions point to a search for knowledge that involves the body. This embodied search in turn points away from an immutable notion of Divinity to one that is in flux, evolving, and discovered through bodied experience.

Theatre in the classroom signals the body as a way of knowing. With the action of taking off our shoes, students change their physicality, stand on common ground, feel the "earth" that supports them.

It is a symbolic way of leaving constraints behind and walking into something new—their creativity. In theatre, students are "allowed" to connect their feelings and ideas, through the body, with those of the classroom, perhaps for the first time.

Simple physical exercises used for theatre "warm ups" transform into explorations of the body as a signpost for the Holy: the stretching of limbs or the deep intake and exhale of a breath. When entered into with awareness, breathing becomes the seed for meditative practice. Opening and closing the hand, and then the entire body, can become a physicalization of isolation and connectivity. Swaying back and forth can offer sensations of mourning, prayer, ecstasy. Mirroring another's actions becomes a silent blessing. Words are not needed. The movement of the body is enough to feel. At the same time, movement is experienced differently by each student. Our lived experiences, held within the body, make it so.

The voice can be a signal for being out of touch with the body. For example, female students sometimes speak in high-pitched tones. Often these same students will make statements, yet they sound like questions. Theatre exercises can work to build confidence and a sense of identity. In chapter 4 we will explore how the use of character work allows students to reinhabit their bodies/voices and find the freedom to express their feelings and opinions. When students enact characters, they "rehearse" how a feeling or an idea is articulated. Just as wearing a mask allows our bodies to bend and jump in ways outside of who we think we are, so when we improvise a character, or enact the words of a character from a text, we express feelings and thoughts beyond a sense of ourselves. In fact, the whole body works with the voice to express. Becoming a character is an occasion for students to grow in confidence at expressing themselves. In the case of female students, the voice becomes less full of air, less high in pitch, and the seeming question mark ending each sentence becomes a period.

Sometimes using theatre, using the body, can awaken memories of joy and of pain. So teacher and student need to enter the religion and theatre journey with care-filled knowledge that the body holds memories. I will address this issue of body and memory in chapter 8 once you have an understanding of my theatre approach.

Yes, theatre is all about bodies. Bodies are texts. Religions are sacred texts. The theatre can be the arena in which we embody these texts.

EXPERIENCE

Experience is that rich fabric that consists of our family histories, cultural upbringing, home and work relationships, emotional histories, education, religious upbringing, everyday spirituality—that which makes each of us who we are. The actor, aware of her own experience, uses this rich fabric in theatre improvisations, scenes, physicalization, mime, and movement. An actor will also use pieces of her lived experience as a resource in creating a character in a play. When I teach acting, actors learn to first share pieces of their own lives before they can learn to enact characters. This is an act of re-membering who we are from our lived experiences. It is a muscle. The more we use it, the stronger it becomes. Giving voice and enacting our stories as well as being heard, reveals and affirms us.

The experiences of our everyday lives are sources of theatre. In beginning acting classes I ask students to create two minutes, silently, from their everyday lives. It always seems to be a temptation for young actors to eschew revealing their ordinariness in favor of creating an exercise with pyrotechnics—jumping off cliffs, hacking through jungles as they hide from an imagined murderer. But the point of the exercise is to give the student space and time to simply be himself in front of an audience doing simple things like reading a newspaper, brushing teeth, washing dishes. It sounds easy, but isn't. Playwrights also bring the experiences of their everyday lives to plays. Emily Shihadeh, a Palestinian American, and I co-authored a play about her life that juxtaposes personal and political history. *Grapes and Figs Are in Season: A Palestinian Woman's Story* relates the daily struggle of the Palestinian people for self-determination and of Emily's everyday life.

> My sister had breast cancer. She needed chemotherapy. She was living in Ramallah, which is just north of Jerusalem. This was during the 7 Days War. She went into Jerusalem and received the chemo from Jewish doctors—at the same time as the Israelis were killing us![8]

Playwright Cherrie Moraga drew upon her Latina identity in her play *Heroes and Saints.* Before she wrote the play, Moraga spent time outside of Bakersfield, California, interviewing Mexican migrant families. The play weaves themes of chemical pollution from pesticides and capitalism's greed with the everyday experiences of a migrant family. The lead female character is a head, an icon of the deformities caused by poisonous pesticides.

Liberation and feminist theologies tell us that doing theology is a second step, that the first step is looking at everyday experience. Theory begins with experience. In my courses, I am keenly interested in looking at the experience of a religion, how it is lived in the everyday, how the everyday is the site of the Holy. What are the daily situations and practices that are inspired by belief? How is belief reflected in how one lives with one's family and neighbors both locally and globally? What are the embodied, visible and audible, sensory manifestations of a religion? Christian feminist liturgies, as well as many Wiccan and Goddess rituals, focus on elements of everyday life. Water, washing, cooking, and real meals are used by Christian feminists for communion rather than symbolic feedings.[9] In African and Native American traditions, the everyday is also invested with the spiritual. Everyday utensils are often beautifully carved with a face of a spirit—art is functional, the spirits exist in everything.

But in the classroom, how we share our lived experiences, and when, are questions of hot debate. As Parker Palmer has suggested:

> If identity and integrity are more fundamental to good teaching than technique—and if we want to grow as teachers—we must do something alien to academic culture: we must talk to each other about our inner lives—risky stuff in a profession

that fears the personal and seeks safety in the technical, the distant, the abstract.[10]

Though Palmer is talking about teachers talking to teachers, I would suggest that in the religious studies classroom the teacher must model the integration of ideas and lived experience. Certainly, it is a question of timing. Several years ago, I began a course on women and religion by telling my spiritual autobiography. That was a mistake. I had laid no groundwork. No community of trust had been built. The following year, I waited until we took up the topic of Christianity, some five weeks into the course. Then my story was heard, not resisted. It was an opening for others to do the same. We had built a community of trust. In subsequent chapters, I will offer theatre methods to assist in building such trust in the classroom.

As an avenue for building community and trust I encourage students to share their experiences with one another. During the first meeting of our "Mystery and Meaning" introductory class, I invite the students to engage in an exercise about our ancestors. The exercise speaks directly to how and how much we choose to share about ourselves. The exercise allows all in the class to "make their experience visible" and become a witness to their own stories. I divide the class into groups of three or four. Each person in the group is asked to " body sculpt," to mold her peers like clay into three living sculptures (sculpting is further explained in chapter 3). The first "three dimensional sculpture" is of her grandparents' notion of mystery and meaning; in the second, she remolds her peers to show her parents' notion, and then in a third she sculpts her own notion of mystery. After each sculpture is created, there are lively discussions within each group. What was that sculpture about? What was your mother doing in the second one? I wasn't clear about that gesture, what was going on? Afterwards, each group selects several sculptures to share with the entire class.

Once the sculptures are shown to the whole group, I direct the discussion to the purpose of the course: What is religious experience? Did you see it depicted in any of these sculptures? And off we go. The living sculptures witness to complexity, vast diversities, and similarities. The exercise is an opportunity on the first day of class to introduce students to theatre and the multiplicity of our religious experiences. When students are invited to do so, I am constantly amazed by how openly they share their lives and view each others' lives with respect. Clearly there is no right or wrong in this exercise. It is simply a matter of choosing what one wants to share.

What students reveal about their own notions of mystery and meaning is also fascinating. Often they depict themselves alone with nature. And conversely, students often depict their grandparents as physically stiff and gender stereotyped, and in Christian cases, carrying a Bible. With discussion, we reflect on their grandparents' everyday struggle to survive, sometimes against great hardship, and how "religion" and religious community provided consistency and often got them through. We then compare students' solitary searches for meaning to that of their ancestors.

Whether we explore our own experiences as the site of the Holy, or explore the experiences of others found in texts, theatre animates, illumines, and encourages empathy for our human divine story. At the beginning of class, students took off their shoes and entered the circle as individuals with histories and stories. In the circle, we begin to see into others' spiritual journeys, noting how the Holy leaves tracks, clues imprinted on everyday life. We listen and reflect on each others' histories and stories. We come into relationship.

RELATIONSHIP

In the teaching universe that I inhabit, the body and lived experience are essential to theatre and religion. I am not in this universe alone. Buber's "I-Thou" is the relational dynamic that inspires me. Being in relation means understanding and accepting the other's identity, realizing our differences, and finding them enriching.

The movement from individual to relationship is one that the theatre typifies. Actors create characters that relate to each other and relate to their world. The acting process is all about relationship.

Relationship for the actor begins when she finds the emotional links between herself and the character. She is creating empathy. Once she finds this, she builds the character's "story," or biography—the character's past history before the play itself begins. This is the actor's "homework" as she prepares for rehearsal with other actors for the play. As the actor is getting to know his character, he starts the process of attending rehearsals. His character meets and interacts with other characters involved in the play's story. This process, too, is an experience of entering into relationship. It may seem like a contradiction that relationship in the theatre is built on an actor's disciplined process of character self-definition—but this work of etching a clear identity determines the richness of the exchange with other characters of the play.

Rehearsals also reveal how mutuality is a key element in relationship. Mutuality means respect and shared power with the other. How that looks in rehearsals is "showing up" at rehearsals: coming prepared to work with a scene partner by having studied the script and character you are portraying, being on time. Mutuality is a way of rehearsing with the other that shows respect, interest, openness, flow. It is a demeanor between actors that says "yes." This is the embodiment of relationship in the rehearsal process.

Plays and their performance embody the stories of brokenness and wholeness in relationship. From such classics as Albee's *Who's Afraid of Virginia Woolf?* and Eugene O'Neill's *Long Day's Journey into Night,* we understand how gender, sexuality, and class tear at the fabric of relationships and slowly unravel them. In the plays of British playwright Caryl Churchill, we witness the relationship of postcolonialism and globalization, families caught in the sociopolitical stranglehold of greed and violence. Anna Deavere Smith's *Twilight* and *Fires in the Mirror* are burning dramatic soliloquies that attest to the U.S. legacy of racism and classism that divides our human family.

Relationship is a key idea in most religious beliefs. The word points to how religions view the human-divine relationship as well as relations with one another. The practice of relationship extends from human beings to the earth and all earth's creatures. How a religion views these relationships reflects its understanding of power: power over, power with, shared power. Carter Heyward is one of the prime spokespersons for mutual relation in the Christian tradition.

> Struggling for mutual relation is how we keep our balance. It is the "how to" of what it means to live in God . . . the Christian vocation is to learn to experience God's power as shared power that belongs to no one alone, no Creator or creature alone, but rather to us all. . . . I am suggesting that we Christians help one another get clear about the radically interdependent character of all creation, in which we humans play significant, but never solo, roles of leadership.[11]

Thich Nhat Hanh's writings and the teachings of Buddhism likewise understand relationship as interdependence. "The forests are our lungs outside of our bodies."[12] This view of nature is not bifurcated or dualistic. Relationship as interdependence is being with, being at peace with the flow of all life.

But in the classroom, how can we teach relationship? Of course we begin with our bodies!

> When we leave the podium and walk around, suddenly the way you smell, the way you move become very apparent to your students. Also, you bring with you a certain kind of potential, though not guaranteed, for a certain kind of face-to-face relationship and respect for "what I say" and "what you say." Student and professor are looking at each other.[13]

When we meet our students face to face, whether in conversation or theatre exercises, we encounter different locations of age, ethnicity, class, and sexual orientation. Mutuality is possible in the meeting. From "what I say" and "what you say," differences can ignite and illuminate. As theologian Nelle Morton said, "we hear each other into speech." And yet, there is no question that creating a relationship with our students is filled with hesitancy, even resistance—on both sides. But the willingness and openness of the teacher is a model for students. When a teacher introduces theatre to students, it can feel like a hand extended, a new avenue opened for students to experience their voices. Something new is possible.

We also see relationship enacted when the student meets a text through his body and enacts that body of knowledge. In a subsequent chapter I will describe students studying the Bhagavad Gita, memorizing portions of it, and enacting the Arjuna-Krishna dialogue.

When a student takes the words of this ancient text into himself, a new relationship is born, the words begin to unlock their meaning, the text speaks to the student. When students give voice to and enact the text, their bodies become the body of knowledge that is also the text. Relation is born through embodiment.

There are many theatre exercises and plays that address aspects of relationship. In subsequent chapters I will offer other examples. Here I will mention two, "mirroring" and "namaste."

Mirroring is participating in Thich Nhat Hanh's flow of interdependence. The class is divided into twos. I model this exercise first with a student. Each person faces the other. They gaze into each other's eyes. Already students can be uncomfortable and resort to laughter. That's okay. It's a way to release tension! As they continue to look into the other's eyes, one person will "lead" by doing simple gestures, slowly. The other mirrors the exact movements. Gradually there is trust that the exercise is not about trickery. Gradually there is silence and pure movement. I ask them, without stopping, to switch "leaders." Again there may be laughter, initial discomfort. But gradually, as the partners are familiar with the exercise, there will be silent flow. You can feel it. Again, without stopping their flow, I ask them to allow leading and following to glide back and forth between them, to keep exchanging roles, as they feel it—perhaps to see if it's possible to have no leader/follower! Through this exercise, the students will experience the give and take of relationship, the process of getting to know, of trusting the other through movement, letting go of one's boundaries, even for a moment. The two may even find themselves breathing together!

Afterwards, I ask the students to reflect on the exercise, to write phrases or word chains. We read them out loud around the circle as we sit on the floor, together. We reflect together about Thich Nhat Hanh's or Carter Heyward's notions of relationship, mutuality, and interdependence, based on the students' experience of this exercise. Sometimes, at another point in the semester, I ask students to do the same exercise again. The reprise of the exercise acts as a kind of personal evaluation for each student of how far he or she has come in trust, concentration, and mutuality.

When we are studying "the one that is not other" in Hinduism, I invite students to experience the feeling of "Namaste," the daily greeting people give to one another in India. The exercise begins with moving about the classroom. When each student meets another, he or she bows slightly, and says "I bow to the God within you" (a loose translation of "namaste"). Each student, depending on the size of the class, says this phrase ten to thirty times! The embodiment of this phrase so many times offers a true experience! The student greets another, and another. Whether they look at each other or shyly whisper to the floor, bowing and saying the words of this ancient greeting is an oral, listening, and physical act that allows each person to briefly experience Hinduism's view of relationship, the one that is not other. At each greeting, the student meets the thoughts and feelings held within the word "namaste." In a subsequent chapter I will elaborate more on memorization, the power that is released when we take the words of a sacred text inside us, when we become one with another's words.

For me, pedagogy in the religious studies classroom is always an exploration of relationship. Theatre allows us the opportunity to experience that relationship, whether we are speaking of human dyads or divine human dyads, or the interdependence of all life. And though the theatre exercise in the classroom is a "taste," a moment in time, its seeds have been planted in students—to bloom another day.

COMMUNITY

One of the reasons I think I create theatre is because it is an opportunity for me to re-create family. I am the oldest of eight children. Today,

I live with my partner. Just the two of us. And like so many others in our individualistic society, I seek ways to be in community. Theatre is a chance to work together, create, struggle, get lost, be found, express as one body something we all want to say. Theatre is a campfire that illuminates the faces of those of us who are gathered around.

Religions and their various codes for dressing, eating, relationship, religious practice at home and temple, calendars of holy days, religious education—set believers apart. Through the body, daily practices, and ways of relating to "the other," religions inscribe their identities/separateness and create their communities. Yet separateness is at once the code to "welcome the stranger," "to love thy neighbor as thyself," to become mindful of our common experience of suffering. The other is none other.

Our bodies, varied life experiences, and relationships with one another are "the stuff" of community. Body, experience, relation reveal the corpus of meaning. Christianity would call this "the mystical body of Christ." This corpus is one body. Gaia. Creation.

But community eludes us. People are torn by political conflict, fractured by cultural, religious, racial, and economic divides. Religion has often been a prime motivator for this violence.

Classrooms must be places where we learn to hold difference and commonalities. Classrooms are opportunities to rehearse, to practice, how we want to live with one another.

The experience of building community in the classroom must begin the first day of classes. We take off our shoes, gather in a circle. What do we hold in common? What will hold our differences? What will keep us from splintering off in many directions? We share a common pursuit of learning, a common intention to use theatre as a method of inquiry, and a question: What is religious experience? Yes, our cognitive, scholarly enterprise will guide and challenge us. But it is the use of theatre methods that will viscerally bind us, one to the other. The use of theatre—embodied imagination, chaos, creativity—will illuminate our commonalities and differences and hold them in trust. Thus community is what is hoped for, the end result of a semester of using theatre. Community is the "not yet," becoming.

During the first few sessions of a course, I introduce several theatre exercises that help to build trust as well as offer models for holding our differences. An initial body sculpture exercise I use on the first day of class offers students an example of their creativity and thus their differences.

In this exercise I ask volunteer students to form improvised "sculptures" of one-word themes: earth, sky, family, mother, father, religion, and finally, God. As they join the exercise one at a time, I direct students to link physically one with the other to form the sculpture. When a student joins a sculpture, he is choosing how his own involvement will complexify the present image. Here are some of the results. To depict earth, some students are flat on the ground; another sits on their prostrate bodies holding a student representing a child. Others spread their limbs as trees. This exercise demands that students rely on one another physically to form an idea.

To depict family, I often see students create a hands-on-the-hips father who points judgmentally at a whimpering child on the ground with the mother, arm linked with father, reaching out to the child. Another child or older sibling often stands next to a parent, smiling, looking straight out at us. When I ask students to create various sculptures of God, several invariably show a "Father God," sans hand on the hips, but pointing, even glaring, at "His" creation. Mother has vanished.

At the end of all the sculptures, we begin to unpack the images: What do you find compelling about them? What felt untrue to you? Was any image similar to another? Why? Students are often surprised by the similarity between the "father" and "God" sculptures. This exercise stirs up student responses. It's important for the teacher to acknowledge all impressions of the sculptures. Students see that multiple interpretations are possible for a simple image. These sculptures are also visceral expressions of bodies making meaning, connecting and interpreting. In this way, theatre is a visceral method for building a community in which we voice our differences as well as our shared concerns, connections, commonality.

The religious studies classroom or the theatre's stage can become the vehicle by which we imagine and rehearse the community we would like to see in the world. As Brazilian theatre director Augusto Boal puts it, "theatre is a rehearsal for revolution." The classroom too, in how we teach what we teach, can be—must be—a rehearsal for building community.

We started with taking off our shoes, pushing the desks back, and gathering in a circle: body, experience, relationship, community. These are the stepping stones of an embodied pedagogy for teaching religious studies. The following chapters will map specific theatre exercises for your classroom. May they be of use to you as we rehearse the world we would like to see.

Namaste.

2

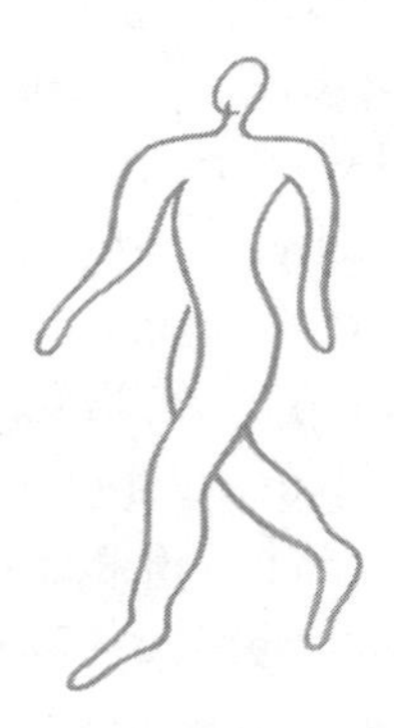

standing on holy ground

Energizing and Focusing the Classroom

IN NOVEMBER 2002, I presented a paper at the American Academy of Religion's National Meeting in Toronto in a session focused on pedagogy. I was the sixth speaker in a seven-person panel. For a panel of so many presenters, it was already a challenge! As I stepped up to the podium, I noticed people dozing off out in the audience. It was time to improvise. I walked off the "stage" into the sea of chairs and invited the audience of seventy-five people to get on their feet. What? Use my body at an academic conference? That is exactly the point! Body knowledge, embodied knowledge, somatic learning. We did shake outs of our arms and legs, tension releasing movements with the neck and shoulders, stretches and yawns, and even backrubs for one another. What a joy it was to see people smiling, wiggling and giggling in delight, laughing and just enjoying themselves. The energy in the room had palpably changed.

Then, I invited volunteers from the audience to create a series of sculptures, physical thematic pictures that use the bodies of several other people (explained in chapter 3). After initial hesitancy, adventuresome souls stepped forward. They created sculptures of "Religion," "G-O-D," and "Pedagogy." I was struck by how playful the professors were! How energized and focused at the task. How well they worked with one another to let something new happen. If my twenty-minute presentation time had permitted, I would have begun a discussion after each of the sculpted images, particularly the final image of pedagogy, since it was the topic of the panel. A discussion prompted by questions like: How does your idea of "pedagogy" match with the sculpture? What title would you give the sculpture? How would you change the image to better communicate its theme? But the clock was ticking and the seventh panel member was still waiting to present his paper. So I "ascended" the podium again, to read a portion of my paper—"Theatre as Pedagogy in the Religious Studies Classroom." The audience was awake now. They were in their bodies. They could hear me.

However you choose to use theatre in your classroom, it must begin on the first day. If you introduce it later in the semester, there will be resistance to theatre used merely as an add-on, rather than an important part of what and how you are teaching. Let me also suggest that your course description should alert students to the use of theatre. I offer an example below for an introductory, 100 level course, entitled "Mystery and Meaning."

> The focus of this course will be to inquire into the nature of religious experience as a way to approach mystery and meaning. We will use theatre to encounter and explore religious experi-

> ence. We will study and enact original texts from Hinduism, Buddhism, Islam, Judaism, and Christianity. We will use theatre techniques and plays to stimulate and provoke conversation on: How should we live? What is religious experience? Plays read will focus on religion (or aspects thereof) and help us navigate spiritual/cultural/religious worlds.

At our first class meeting, students know to expect something new. They come hoping for it, actually. There are some thirty students present. We meet once a week for three hours. I find that my approach demands more than the eighty minutes twice-weekly approach of most courses. I'd asked for a big clear, carpeted room and moveable chairs. But all that was available was this small auditorium with bolted down seats and a small raised lecturing area, carpeted, at the front of the room. That's where we gathered. It was a little tight. You make do. On the "holy ground" of creativity, we take off our shoes. There's something leveling about everyone being in socks or barefoot as the case may be. Leveling. That's a good word to describe what theatre is doing on the first day of a class—bringing us all together on the same ground level.

We begin with exercises that energize the body. I find these exercises are helpful to make the transition between what students are coming from and what they are about to do. The physical activities are important even if you follow them with traditional activities like sitting and engaging in conversation. The exercises help us to focus our energies and concentrate more fully. I remind the students that there are many ways of "knowing." We are beginning with our bodies.

In addition to exercises that energize the body, this chapter offers vocal exercises that call forth the range of the human voice. Taken as a whole, the methods awaken the voice as both metaphor and reality for "finding our voices." Practically, they help students gain confidence in the sound and power of their own voices.

Throughout the chapter there are group exercises because it is important in a classroom to create community. Group work fosters a "communal body." Through group movement without words and group vocalizing, as well as work in dyads, students build trust in one another and generate a spirit of fun and enjoyment. Work in groups also builds confidence for subsequent individual exercises.

To use any of the exercises most effectively in the classroom, keep these overall suggestions in mind:

- *Emphasize self-knowledge.* It's important in beginning sessions to tell students that they know their bodies best. Thus if an exercise is a physical hardship or causes pain of any kind, don't do it. You know your body best. (In past years I have had students with various disabilities. I encourage them to do as much of the work as they are able. Students with other physical issues either speak to me before class or during office hours. What matters most is communication and a willingness to try).
- *Provide introductions.* When I introduce theatre exercises, I like to give them a context beforehand. For example, "We are on the holy ground of creativity—please take off your shoes." Or "We are all coming from hectic schedules and other situations prior to this class. One way to shed that baggage and begin a new focus is theatre exercises. They engage our bodies and create a clean slate."
- *Give verbal positive support.* Present a positive supportive attitude for your students as they encounter these exercises. This will encourage them to stick with the work.

EXERCISES TO AWAKEN BODY, VOICE AND MIND

The following exercises are offered to awaken the body, voice, and mind. You can use them to energize the classroom before you move to a topic. You can also select an exercise to embody a particular idea. I've noted how I do this in boxes that follow some exercises.

Centering: Experience the Stillness

This exercise begins to strengthen the "muscles" of concentration and awareness—qualities that students can use in many settings. It also introduces students very simply, but profoundly, to an awareness of their bodies.

Stand in a circle, on both feet, hands at your sides, and close your eyes. Feel the floor supporting you, your legs supporting you, the trunk of your body supporting you.

Become aware of your breathing. Feel the breath as it passes in and out of your nostrils. Let any sounds outside the classroom be in the background of your awareness. In the foreground, let your focus be to feel the breath moving in and out of your nostrils.

Let the foreground breathing and the background sounds continue as long as it feels comfortable to you. Invite the students to slowly open their eyes. Ask them to notice the obstacles they encountered to standing still, closing their eyes. Ask them just to notice, not to make judgments. When you use this exercise again in the next class session, ask the students to notice how the exercise was different for them than the first time.

Prajna (integrated awareness) Breathing, or Alternate Nostril Breathing

It is best to model this exercise before you ask your students to do it. This yoga breath work is an alternative to the previous exercise and can be used by students to relax, balance, and focus their energies prior to doing another exercise. The exercise works to consciously regulate and balance the physical breathing rythmn of the nostrils. This affects the energy and the mind.

Students sit with an upright spine and closed eyes. Use the fingers to block off one nostril and inhale with the other nostril. Release the blocked off nostril and exhale by blocking the other (inhaled) nostril. Then repeat. It is a circle. This can be repeated five times, and then reverse the process, starting with the opposite side.

Another method of alternate nostril breathing that is easy to understand (when written down like this) is to exhale and inhale from one nostril five times. Then, do five times with the other nostril. That is called a "round." Doing three rounds constitutes a complete practice.

This physical act has an effect on the autonomic nervous system, and allows the student to become "centered" in such a way that both nostrils are flowing smoothly. In this state, the mind is relaxed.

How I use this exercise

In general I use these exercises to bring a quiet focus to the group before we begin the work of the day. Specifically, I use them when addressing Hinduism and Buddhism. With awareness we breathe together. In Buddhism, we enter the "present moment." This experience of the "present moment" can connect directly to the assigned reading, *Being Peace* by Thich Nhat Hanh. Afterwards, we discuss how students experienced the exercise. Their bodied experience is our entrance into the topics of what is awareness, the present moment, and being peace.

Student Responses

A student once said, "I don't like to close my eyes." To which I responded, "That's fine, Theresa. You can visually focus on something—your shoe. Try just looking at your shoe. How does that feel?" "Fine." And with this we went on with the exercise.

•

BODY WARM-UPS: AWAKENING THE BODY

Isn't it amazing that we think we can learn anything by simply applying our minds to the task? With an awakened body, our blood is flowing, doing its work of energizing and refreshing our interior landscapes, including the brain! We begin with body awareness exercises that both energize and relax.

Shake-outs

Isolating parts of the body while trying to maintain relaxation in the rest of the body is helpful for building focus and energy.

Extend your right arm into the circle. Shake the hand vigorously—not the arm, just the hand—as if you were trying to shake off your hand. I always chide my students not to worry—it won't drop off. Continue shaking the hand vigorously. Raise your right arm above your head—shaking, shaking. Now out in front of you again. Now drop your arm at your side. If your hand is not tingling, you're not doing it hard enough. Okay, start the process again, this time with your left hand. Same thing. Now move the shake out to your right ankle and foot. Balance on your left leg. Shake your right foot—but shake it from the right ankle. Do the same for the left foot.

After introducing this exercise, I complicate it by asking students to: shake the right hand and left foot, or shake the left hand and left foot, or left hand and right foot, etc. It takes everyone a moment to adjust their thinking, but it's fun and provides laughter.

Tension Release Exercises

Tension blocks energy flow. Each of these exercises helps release tension. Use them together or pick and choose.

Bring your shoulders to your ears—breathe in as you do this. Release your shoulders, exhaling. Do this three times (see Figure 1).

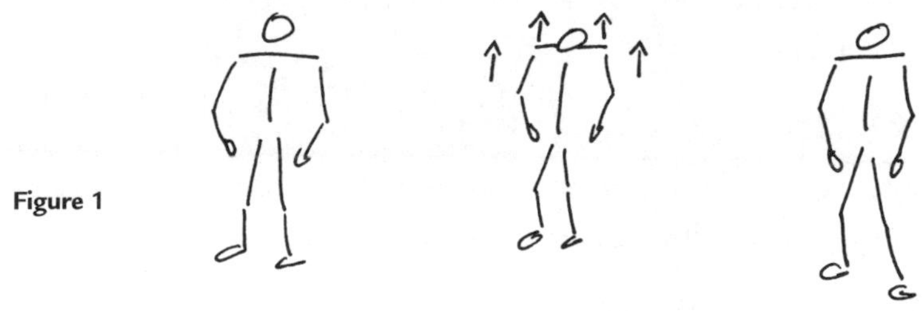

Figure 1

Crouch and make your body as small as you can. Then release the position by bouncing into an upright position, arms and legs extended wide. Crouch as you breathe in. Exhale as you extend wide. Do this several times. (see Figure 2).

Allow your head to drop forward; inhale and exhale. Bring your head/neck to center. Let the head drop to the right. Inhale and exhale.

Figure 2

Bring the head/neck to center. Let the head/neck drop back, and let the jaw drop open. Inhale and exhale. Bring the head/neck to center. Let the head/neck drop to the left. Inhale and exhale. Bring the head/neck to center. Repeat in the opposite direction (see Figure 3).

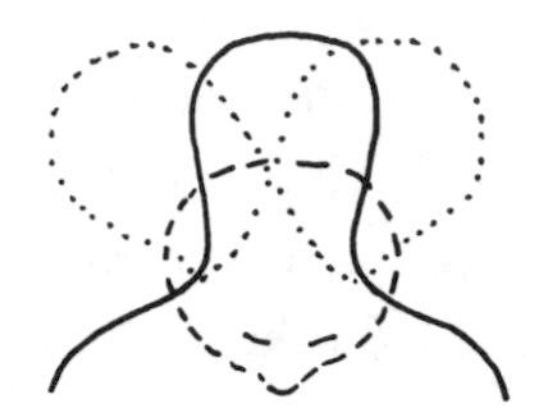

Figure 3

Salutation to the Sun

Yoga is the union of breath and body movement. In India and elsewhere it is a form of bhakti, devotion. Along with some of the warm ups listed here, I use it regularly to begin classes. A regular physical warm up is a consistent pattern that students like. The Salutation to the Sun opens the mind and heart, unleashes energy, wakes up the spine and provides alertness. Knowing that breathing and movement can be devotion, with use, students can grow into the experience of the exercise.

There are many different versions of the "Salutation to the Sun." I would suggest that you find it on the internet or attend a yoga class and discover which version you like best for yourself.[1]

WHOLE GROUP EXERCISES: BUILDING TRUST AND COMMUNITY

The classroom is a rehearsal for a world we would like to see. In the classroom we can create trust, peace, harmony, a respect for cultural and religious differences. Group exercises hold differences and commonalities in trust. Particularly at the beginning of a semester, group exercises offer seeds for community. In this pedagogy, community building is visceral. With the bodied exercises that follow, students interact and play with one another. They laugh. All are involved, including the teacher. Each student can relax and simply be part of the group. Boundaries are loosened. Trust begins. When trust is present, it waters and makes supple the ground of learning. Once the seeds of community are planted, students are able to stand up with less fear and offer presentations, alone or in dyads, in front of the class.

Mirror the Movement

Individuals become one body as the whole group moves to the music. At the same time, individuals initiate movements to the music, thus offering their own interpretations. This exercise can be used as a warm-up to raise the energy of the group. It can also be used to experience the dynamics between individual creativity and community membership. There is extraordinary beauty in this exercise. Students connect and interpret an outside stimulus (music), make it their own through gestures and movement, and then communicate it to the group. The entire group mirrors the movement/gesture and kinesthetically we begin to bond, to create community. What one person does affects the entire group. How the community responds to each movement affects the individual. Community consciousness and connectivity is fostered, as well as creativity.

Make a circle with the class. Put on music. I use Ruben Blades, or "Carmina Burana" by Carl Orff, or the "Missa Luba," something that has many rhythms in it. The first leader responds to the music by starting a rhythmic gesture (e.g., perhaps the music inspires you to move your arms in large circles, as in Figure 4). Ask students to mir-

Figure 4

ror exactly what you are doing. Make the movements simple and repetitive, and not too fast so that they can easily follow you. When it feels right, point to another person in the circle and ask that person to lead. He or she can do anything, as long as it's easy to follow. Encourage each leader not to think about it—just respond to the music. Coach them to use their entire bodies in the movements. This exercise can go on as long as you'd like—but probably not beyond ten minutes. Leaders will begin to feel free and even lead the group around the room, others will have us get on the ground, still others will want us to widen and then shrink the circle.

At a certain point, let the circle go and invite the students to move about the room working with the rhythms of the music. That's right, just dance and enjoy yourselves!

How I use this exercise

Primarily I use this exercise at the beginning of a semester to foster community in the classroom. It energizes the class, to "get us all on the same page." I use it following the body warm-ups listed above because this exercise is also done in a circle and asks individual students to do movement in front of the whole circle of classmates—perhaps for the first time in our class sessions. Because of this, I find myself coaching during the exercise—encouraging students to "use your whole body! It's more fun! Get your legs involved!"

Student Respones

Students react in various ways: a shy young woman, sometimes in rhythm, sometimes not, will raise an arm and brush the hair from her brow, giggle, and say "I can't"—the group mirrors these exact gestures and we go on; some adventurous young men will do splits or handstands—we all groan and do our best to mirror what we can and then we go on. Whatever is offered by individuals, we mirror.

Effect on the rest of the class

What is the effect on the rest of the class? Laughter. Joking. Moving our bodies to rhythms together. We share a common ground that comes from accomplishing the exercise. We discuss what we have experienced and relate it to the word "community:" shared intentions/goals, mutual respect, appreciation for each person's creativity and interpretation. Following this, we talk about the kind of atmosphere we would all like to foster in the community of the classroom.

•

Walking A Mile In Another's . . .

This exercise allows students to viscerally experience the physicality of "the other." It allows students to break their "normal" way of moving through space. When habitual movement is broken, we notice things. When we move our bodies in new ways, in our mind's eye we also feel and sense new things. A new body position can introduce us to how it might feel to inhabit another body different from our own.

When we do this exercise we bring consciousness to movement. We also bring intention to movement, such as breathing with awareness. Awareness can help us to sense the power of our actions.

Put on soft, focusing, background music.

Ask the students to walk about the classroom at their own speed, not making contact with anyone else, being conscious of their breathing. Bring awareness to how the air moves around you as you move through space, breathing and walking.

Ask students to walk as quickly as they can around the room, without running, without talking. Abruptly, tell them to walk as slowly as possible, slow motion, but still keep moving. Now switch, as fast as they can. Switch again, as slowly as possible.

Note: There will be students who want to make extreme movements to this entire exercise. As long as they are doing the work, I encourage all ranges of responses. In fact such behavior, when kept within the boundaries of the exercise, can stimulate the energy of others and even be boldly creative.

Ask the students to continue walking at a comfortable speed, but now on their toes. Then add walking on your toes with little tiny steps, then large steps, then as fast as they can, then as slowly as they can.

Coaching: Notice how your entire body is affected by walking in different rhythms on your tiptoes.

Coaching: As you move in ways that you don't usually move, let images of other people, or animals that move this way come into your mind. Just notice them. Are there feelings attached to these movements? Notice them.

Have students release walking on their toes and continue neutral walking.

Ask students to walk with their shoulders hunched forward and their head down (see Figure 5a).

Figure 5a

Coaching: Are there feelings attached to this posture?

Ask students to walk, with their shoulders hunched forward and heads down, as fast as they can without running. Then, with the same posture, have them walk as slowly as they can.

Release walking with this posture; ask students to continue neutral walking.

Have students do this same process in walking with:

- extending forward the chest, and then the stomach, and then both (see Figure 5b).
- walking with toes turned out (see Figure 5c).
- walking on the heels, head and chin up (see Figure 5d).

  Coaching: Notice what it feels like to look down on something.
- walking with hands on hips and taking giant steps (see Figure 5e).
- trying combinations of the above.

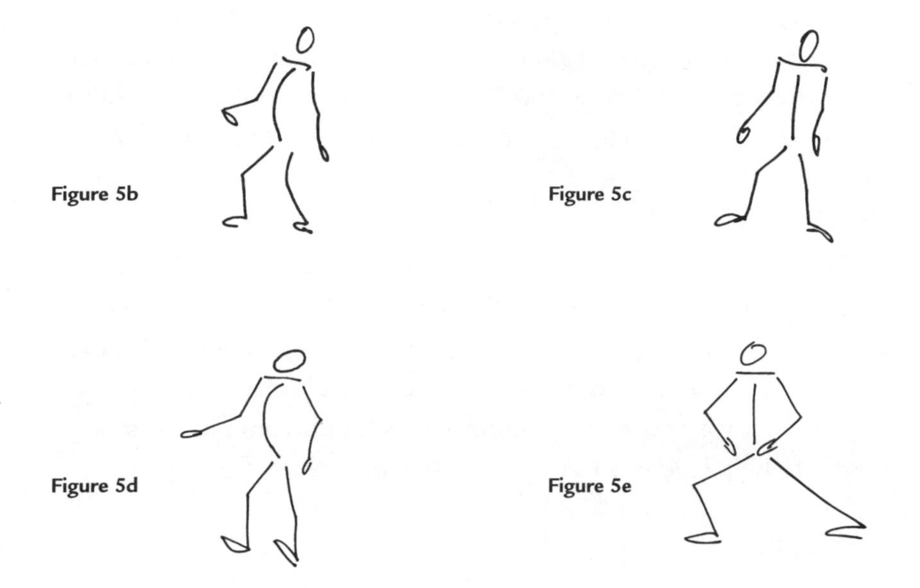

Figure 5b

Figure 5c

Figure 5d

Figure 5e

Coaching: Notice that there are feelings with all of the body positions.

Discussion Points

- How is your bodied experience of these exercises different from when you walk down the street? Do you bring consciousness and intention to your everyday walking?
- If experiencing the body can be a way of knowing, what do you learn from these exercises? (you may also want to add a free-write exercise that students only share with you)
- In the "Mirror the Movement Exercise," what did you learn about this group?
- In the "Walking a Mile in Another's . . . " did the various physical positions and rhythms remind you of certain animals? Did the various movements remind you of people that you know? How is gender, age, race/ethnicity, sexuality related to any of these movements? Through the movements, did you discover stereotypes? What is a stereotype? When someone moves differently than we do, what is the urge in us to label and judge?

- In the "Walking a Mile in Another's . . ." take one physicality (e.g., hunched shoulders, head down) and recall how it made you feel. Create a character from those feelings in your imagination. Write a monologue by that character describing "one day in my life."

How I use this exercise

The experience of empathy can be a result of this exercise. When I focus on the principle of welcoming the stranger in Judaism, and the Christian principle of "love your neighbor as yourself," I use this exercise to stimulate discussion about who is the other. In my biblical drama class, we create contemporary characters from biblical stories. I use it to help students learn to imagine and create characters.

Student Responses

"I've learned to use movement to explore feelings."

"It helped me to not be afraid or judgmental with people who are different from me."

"If somebody had asked me if I love my neighbor, I would have said sure. But moving my body, I had to look much deeper."

•

VOICE WARM-UPS

In our world, people are sometimes referred to as "without a voice," for example the homeless, people living in poverty, and other marginalized populations. "Having a voice" is associated with empowerment: and identity, the ability to name one's circumstances, possessing power, and the methods to influence power.

Our voices are signatures. Kristen Linklater's work exemplifies this when she speaks of "liberating the natural voice." She describes the voice as being capable of expressing emotions, textures, and moods within a two-to-four octave natural pitch range.

> The objective is a voice in direct contact with emotional impulse, shaped by the intellect but not inhibited by it. Such a voice is a built-in attribute of the body with an innate potential for a wide pitch range, intricate harmonics and kaleidoscopic textural qualities, which can be articulated into clear speech in response to clear thinking and the desire to communicate. The natural voice is transparent—revealing, not describing, inner impulses of emotion and thought, directly and spontaneously. The *person* is heard, not the person's voice.[2]

Put another way, our voices reflect being at home in ourselves. As I described in chapter 1, some young women have high-pitched voices that seem to make every statement into a question and some young men have booming voices that seem to form every statement into a command. To assist students to find the power of their voices, exercises in this section will engage the full vocal range.

Perhaps a voice is breathy or very soft. The "Waking Up" exercise fills the diaphragm with air to support sound generation. It will also offer awareness of new vocal ranges. In "Waking up the Mouth" and "Unique New York," the point is articulation rather than loudness. Later on, these exercises can be used as vocal preparations for working with texts.

A voice, when blended or contrasted with other voices, can be a thrilling experience of unity, beauty, and power. We can also find our individual voices by being a part of a group voice. The "Sounding" exercise offers an opportunity to build vocal confidence, trust, cooperation, and unity in a group setting.

Waking Up

This exercise opens the throat and awakens the vocal chords.

Stand upright. Stretch as if you were waking up. Open your mouth wide and yawn, using your voice, as if sighing. Encourage students to be irreverent—not to hide the yawn. Do the same process again. This time, begin the vocal part of the yawn at a high pitch and let the sound of the vocal yawn slide to the lowest possible note. Repeat this three times.

Thinking Cap[3]

The exercise helps students wake up, helps to focus attention on hearing, relaxes tension in the cranial bones, and increases voice resonance.

The student uses thumbs and index fingers to pull the ears gently back and unroll them. Begin at the top of the ear and gently massage down and around the curve, ending with the bottom lobe. Keep the head upright, chin level. Repeat the process three or more times.

Wake Up the Mouth

This exercise sensitizes the mouth and is particularly good to do before speaking a text.

Take a deep breath from the diaphragm. Blow out the lips (your nose will tickle as your lips vibrate). Do it with energy. Bite the lips. Bite the tongue. Gently! Repeat this three times.

Unique New York

In this exercise I'm looking for articulation and have chosen words with good consonants. You might choose another phrase that is more local to personalize the exercise.

Repeat slowly and then increase the pace, "unique New York."

Coaching: Make the start and finish of each word clear. Overdo the movements of your mouth.

Repeat slowly and then increase the pace: "I need and love unique New York."

Coaching: Again, make the start and finish of each word clear. Overdo the movements of your mouth.

Walk about the room, easily, and speak this phrase to the walls—softly, then loudly.

Coaching: Hear the sound of your voice and that of others in the room.

Sounding

Sounding is at once a visceral experience of both the beauty and power of the individual voice and the group voice. You will find yourself getting light-headed in a comfortable way. This "high" feeling comes from working with long sustained breaths and vocal tones. You will experience the power of a highly focused vocal activity. The exercise offers an aural method to building community.

In setting up the exercise, you might tell students that it is an improvisation, like jazz.

Once you have established a tone, and others have matched it, new harmonies and tones can be introduced along side the original tone.

All close their eyes, standing in a circle. The leader takes a deep breath and exhales a sustained tone. The students match it. The tone is not forced, but easy. It can vary in loudness or softness. Everyone will have different lengths of breath that he or she brings to the tone. The important thing is for the group to sustain the tone. For a moment there is nothing else in the world but this one sound! Enter the experience. You will feel its power.

Coaching: Hear your voice. Let it blend with others.

Once this tone is established, the leader or others introduce other tones that are harmonies or melodies. It becomes an improvisation.

Coaching: Keep your eyes closed. You are listening and sounding. Make your own contribution to the group sound, add your own melody or tone, but keep matching and mixing your tone with those of others.

To end the exercise, let the tones slowly get softer or stop. This sometimes can be initiated by the leader, but can also happen organically. The journey of sounding and coming to a finish is very much *what happens.*

Writing Response

Often after exercises that I feel have been strong experiences for students, I ask them to immediately sit and write about it—in phrases, one word per line, narratives, or poetry. Let them choose. You may want them to divide into groups to share their writing, or ask volunteers to read their responses. When a student reads aloud, encourage him or her to recall the articulation exercise of "unique New York"—to start and finish his or her words yet still keep the flow of the sentences.

Discussion Points

- What does it mean to be "voiceless?"
- How does someone "find" their voice?
- How does listening to another help a person to find his or her voice?[4]
- What is the relationship between voice and power?

How I use these exercises

Before students present memorized texts, I have them do the various vocal warm ups in this section as well as body warm ups. This helps to dispel their nervousness and concentrates their energies. I use the Sounding exercise in my class "Enacting Mysticism" as a visceral experience of being lifted to another plane of consciousness, feeling the loss of boundaries in the weave of sounds. I ask students to write about their feelings during the exercise. Afterwards, in the discussion, we draw comparisons to various definitions of mysticism.

•

IDENTITY AND RELATIONSHIP: EXERCISES THAT INTEGRATE BODY, VOICE, AND MIND

"Name and Gesture" offers an experience of inhabiting your name both vocally and with movement. "Mirror" is a surprising experience of respect, intimacy, and mutuality. When it works, students who have worked with each other in the exercise will have a special bond the entire semester.

Name and Gesture

This exercise is excellent for learning students' names, bringing laughter to the classroom, and strengthening student concentration, observation, listening, and somatic memory skills. I do the exercise once a week for the first two weeks.

In a circle, the leader begins by saying her name, then repeating it with a gesture. The whole group then mirrors her movements and sound. The exercise is the most fun when: 1) the gestures are large and involve the whole body, 2) you use each syllable of your name with a gesture, for example, using my own name: Vic—toooooooo—ria!! (see Figure 6)

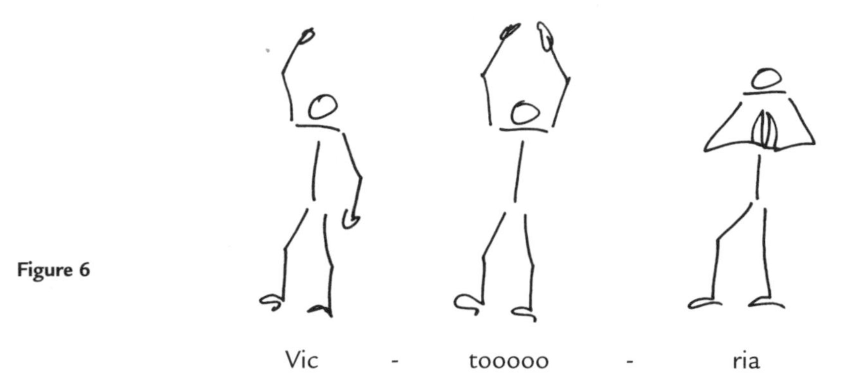

Figure 6

Go around the circle, student by student. Each one will create gestures for his or her name. And with each new name, the group mirrors the name/gesture. Stop every three or four persons and go back, starting with the leader's name/gesture and see if the whole group can repeat the names/gestures.

If a student is shy, any little movement or shy giggle as that person says his or her name is enough—the group can mirror that. When the group mirrors the shy student, it actually allows the shy or resisting student to feel encouraged by the group.

Mirror

This exercise definitely needs modeling by the teacher with a student. The point of this exercise is not to try to trick your partner, but rather to work together. One guides the other. If done with concentration, the two students will feel that they are moving as one body.

To model this exercise, stand facing the other person. Decide who will lead, and thus who will follow. Throughout the exercise it is important to maintain eye contact with your partner. Using your peripheral vision and maintaining eye contact, begin a gesture. (If you are doing this with younger students, have the leaders choose an everyday ritualistic activity, such as brushing your teeth or hair, waving to a friend, or washing the dishes—see Figure 7). *You must keep the eye contact at all times during the exercise.* Let the gestures be as abstract or reality-based as you wish. The point is to keep your partner with you.

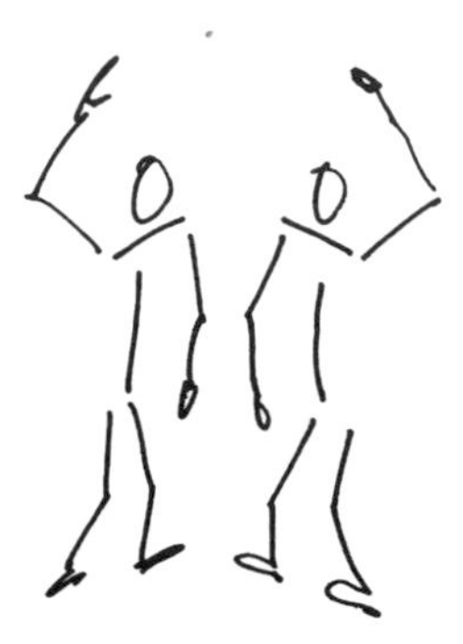

Figure 7

Divide the class in pairs, preferably people who don't know each other. Depending on the age of the students, you might need to match gender. Once they decide who will lead and who will follow, ask them to begin. You'll notice a lot of giggling and talking since people aren't used to looking at each other for this length of time. Encourage them to do the exercise without talking. You will notice that by the time you switch leaders, the students will be concentrated and the nervous giggles and laughter will subside.

Coaching: Concentrate on your gestures. Do the exercise without talking. Keep the eye contact. Slow down your movements. Simplify your movements. Keep your partner with you.

(It's also important to support the couples who are working well with one another: "Good! Nice work! Yes, that's it.")

Eventually you will ask them, mid-gesture, to freeze their movements and switch leaders.

After a time, challenge the couples to continue their gestures, but this time no one is leading or following. Can they "tune in" to each other and move seamlessly together? Slowly! As you walk around the room, can you tell who is leading?

At the end of the exercise, ask each of the partners to find a gesture to thank the other without words. Then let the two of them sit down and discuss the experience.

Writing Response

Next, ask students to write single words per line or phrases per line about their experience of the exercise. Have volunteers share their writing with the class.

Discussion Points

- When you saw and heard everyone repeat your name and gesture, what did you learn about identity?
- Mirror exercise: In some cultures, sustained eye contact is considered rude. How did it work for you?
- What is relationship and how did you see it at work in the mirror exercise? When was it not relationship?
- What have you learned about leading and following from this exercise?
- What does mutuality have to do with the mirror exercise?

• • •

At the University of the Redlands, Fran Grace taught a course entitled "Religion and Hate." In it she used the mirror exercise, which she had learned in a workshop I'd taught for professors. Fran explains, "We were dealing with the role of religion in race conflicts. I invited the students to do the mirror exercise with someone in class they didn't know. A black woman paired with a white man. He found it difficult to follow her when it was her turn to lead. They both said it was hard for them to look into the eyes of the other. Basically, they had great difficulty trusting and being in sync. Their honesty coming out of this exercise (which required their *bodies* to reveal what their *minds* would not in cognitive or discursive learning) led to a heated and meaningful class discussion about racial difference and fear."[5] What Fran discovered with her two students, a black woman and a white man, was resistance. That resistance on the part of each person had complex roots. Each, somewhere in her and his lives, experienced cause not to trust "the other." It is probable that within that experience race, gender, and power differences were important factors. In a classroom discussion, not using the mirror exercise, everyone may have acknowledged race conflicts, perhaps even their own racism, intellectually. But the mirror exercise, both gently and concretely, offered participants an "in-class," live experience. With these two people, their eyes resisted making contact, they found it difficult to "mirror" (read, follow) the other. The exercise exposed the feelings connected to their lived experience. In the exercise, they could not ignore those feelings. The rest of the class benefited as well from their honesty in the discussion.

• • •

The mirror exercise is usually a unifying experience for students. For these two people, it was not. The exercise is about leading and following, as well as trusting the other. It offers visual eye contact that feels like intimacy and trust. But that was impossible given the histories of these two students. The students voiced their struggle with the exercise. The discussion became gritty and difficult, became true.

The topic and discussion of race conflict began with body knowledge. It began nonverbally. Words were a second step, instead of the first.

CONCLUSION

Teaching with the body, exercising the body, learning from our bodies, experiencing a communal body: these are the initial footprints along the path of *Acting Religious.* There are countless other theatre exercises for energizing, focusing, and creating trust and relationship.[6]

When you create some of these exercises in your classroom, I know you may feel you are stepping out onto a windy cliff. But the fresh air from your first flight will be exhilarating and inspire you to do more!

From this chapter, you and your students have experienced theatre exercises that integrate body, voice, and mind. Let us remind ourselves that we are doing this in a religious studies or theology classroom. That the body and voice are part of the learning experience of religion and theology signifies a shift, a seismic shift, away from total reliance on cognitive, discursive forms of pedagogy. Where but in the study of religions and belief should there be recognition that learning is a whole body experience? Where but in the study of religions and belief should there be an understanding that the body is a topography upon which religious practices occur? Learning with the whole self is also an affirmation of the many ways in which students learn. Most of all, this approach to pedagogy is subversive, for within its practices are imbedded visions for reimagining how theologies and religious studies are understood and taught. The methods presented in this book demand of theologians and scholars a recognition that the bodied experience of women and men in everyday life is where belief and religion are realized and tested. To teach religious studies and theology as a solely intellectual pursuit is to miss experiencing the Holy in the earth, in its creatures, and in one another. To miss this is an act of impoverishment for pedagogy. I believe that the integration of body, voice, and mind found in this chapter mirrors the experience of the Holy in the earth body, and in voices of all creation. Theatre in the religious studies or theology classroom reveals that we are human divine creatures. Through this method we catch glimpses of the Holy in gestures, bodies in movement, and our own voices.

3

what's in a story? what's in an image?

Opening Classroom Discussion with Theatre

IT WAS THE THIRD MEETING of my introductory course to religious studies. We began this section on oral religions with improvising a creation story. The students have read a chapter from Lynda Sexson's *Ordinarily Sacred,* the chapter entitled "The First Act Repeated: Myth and Contemporary Consciousness."[1] It is an illuminating story of Lynda working with children in a Unitarian congregation to create and improvise a Christmas play. But because these children are from nontraditionalist families, their Christmas play turns into a humorous romp of gods, angels, and creatures all colliding in time and space. The myth they create is both new and ancient.

I wondered what college students might do with a similar assignment. We sat in a circle, some on the floor, some on chairs.

"Today," I said, "we will improvise our own creation story." Most creation stories begin from nothing. But in fact there is always something there. So I asked the students, what was there in the beginning? Darkness? A sound? A rhythm?

The students replied, "Wind! In the beginning there was wind!"

"And what did it sound like?" Wind sounds circulate around the circle.

"And then what happened?" I ask.

"There were swirls of wind and the wind divided into five swirls!"

"And then what happened?"

"And these swirls called themselves—wanderers. And they swirled around in space."

I waved for volunteers. With the wind sounding, five different students got up and began to twirl and turn about the circle, one in a mechanized wheel chair.

"I am light!" said one. And then, "I am darkness! I am crashing waves! I am rocks and pebbles! I am all sea creatures!"

"And then what happened?"

One of the wanderers said, "Then they split into good and evil!" Two snarled backward, while the others did joyful leaps.

Another wanderer said, "The wanderers fought amongst themselves." Shouts and clamoring, pulling each other to the ground, pouncing one on another.

The student in the wheelchair seemed to almost put her chair into overdrive as she pushed out from the rest of the group, which was caught in shouting and laughing, and moved out beyond our circle. From the other side of the room, she announced, "I am faith, faith in peace and beauty."

The others hoot at her, except for one—darkness. That wanderer says, "And from the brow of faith out popped two humans."

A male and female student from the edge of the circle lept to their feet and joined the action.

The wanderer who was crashing waves said, "The humans grew food from the earth, and lived alongside the animals in harmony."

"That was the way it was supposed to be," said faith.

The wanderer of darkness added, "But just like us, the humans began to war against one another too."

Two more students joined the fray, growling and clawing at the others. The wanderer who was rocks and pebbles said, "But into this mess, a special human was born."

The wanderer of light said "And his name was Jesus and he spoke about peace."

A student from the circle joined the story and stood in the center, still. The wanderer of darkness replieds, "But the Romans came along, and f—ed up all that shit. The end."

"Is that the end?" I asked.

"Yes," they laughed, "unfortunately."

Throughout this chapter we look at methods to open classroom discussions of a topic. I've included stories about my teaching in the hope that you will see how theatre exercises can engage students and become catalysts for discussion.

One difference between the contemporary myth enacted above and those created by oral religions is our comic self-consciousness. These students found that play freed them from mythic models they grew up with—to a point. When chaos appeared the first time with the wanderers, the creation of faith set humans in motion and balance was restored, for a time. When chaos appeared again, this time with humans, a special human wanderer offered peace. And here they seemed to revert to a familiar mythic model, the cycle of chaos—order—chaos. Disharmony reigned at the end of the story. Yet there was laughter in this moment. It was as if humor could lift them above the disorder, seeing it as the human conundrum, cyclical, transparent, goofy. Yet the ending could also be viewed as completely cynical, reflecting a view of the world in which the "big players/Romans" continue to create havoc for those on the margins of power. Inventing myths is the way we look into our own experience.

Improvisation is the creative process of enacting a moment or a story without a set text. Through using the tool of improvisation, students experienced how creation stories evolve. While the exercise seems like a group effort, it is put into motion by individuals creating what the group reinforced. No one was able to offer a whim without the group joining in, resonating, embodying the idea. And where was the instructor? As the teacher/coach, I helped to set the parameters of the form and coached from the side. My role was to witness their process. The story was theirs, not only made from their own intuitions and memories of creation stories, but also a comment on the world as they perceived it. The discussion that followed bridged the short leap to understanding the need in indigenous cultures to speak their visions of their world, and how mythmaking offers identity.

SCULPTURES: IMAGES THAT OPEN DISCUSSION

When religions address daily life, they offer spiritual practices to assist in acceptance and healing from human experiences such as death and dying. And so, depending on the time of year I teach my introductory course, I begin our discussion of Judaism with looking at a personal response to death by Leonard Bernstein (students arrive having read selections from Judith Plaskow's *Standing Again at Sinai* and Abraham Heschel's *Between God and Man: An Interpretation of Judaism*).[2] I give the students the words to Bernstein's "Kaddish" (the mourner's song of praise to God).[3] After reading it, we put on the music. Without discussion, once the last notes are played, I ask a volunteer to create a sculpture of the human-divine relationship heard in Bernstein's work.

In one class, a male student selected four students and moved them into an image. Three students cowered on the floor, and a fourth stood on a chair pointing down at them.

"Good!" I said. "How does this image change in the lyrics? Will someone else come up and create another sculpture?"

A female student created this image: she moved the God figure from the chair to weep in the arms of one of the cowering figures.

"Excellent. Now, can we have another volunteer show us how this image also changes in the lyrics?"

A male student created this image: two male figures stand facing each other, hands on the other's shoulders.

Afterwards, we discussed the various images. Some students disagreed with the sculptures shown. I asked them to create new sculptures and then explain why. In the midst of this we began to discuss the human-divine relationship in Judaism in light of Bernstein, Heschel, and Plaskow.

Teaching has to be a courageous act. In the search to communicate to and with our students, we try many methods. The courage comes in reaching out to something new beyond our comfort borders. It's my belief that today's students are used to learning in various and often simultaneous modalities. They expect it. They expect to see visuals, listen to lectures, network with in-class computers—and some even try covertly to send and receive text messages on telephones at the same time! But what students don't expect is to use their imaginations in a physical way in the name of learning. That's where the courage to teach is involved (thank you, Parker Palmer!). To offer students a new way of learning is a courageous act.

The Kaddish story above sketches a situation in which students are encouraged to value their individual interpretations of a piece of art. A direct line can be drawn, I think, from students' confidence in their imaginations and embodied imaginings to students' courage to express and explore their own thinking about a reading or a topic. If they are involved physically in the classroom, they are involved mentally. If they couple their imaginations with bodied expression, they will sharpen their intellectual engagement.

While this chapter will look at several bodied approaches to beginning a classroom discussion, I will focus primarily on "sculpting." The theatre exercise of "sculpting" creates a three-dimensional image with our bodies. In the Kaddish story above, one student worked with other bodies as if they were clay (the manipulation of arms, legs, faces, etc). She used her imagination and intellect. There are other approaches to build an image/sculpture that I will also discuss in this chapter.

Silence, image, movement, and gesture can be gifts to our wordy classrooms.

Whether it is the Kaddish, Bhagavad Gita, or a sura of the Qur'an, sculpting can be a wordless entry into a text. Imaging is bodied learning, an experience of a body in cooperation with other bodies. It is an opportunity for students to create their own interpretations of a text and from which a discussion can begin. Thus, sculpting an image puts agency in the hands of students. And finally, students like watching other students work. The result: peer interest peaks.

There are many versions of sculpting. One of the most compelling for me is Augusto Boal's "Image Theatre." Boal is the Brazilian theatre activist who developed Theatre of the Oppressed (his book has the same title).[4] Boal's work began as agit prop (agitation propaganda—improvised street theatre in response to social/political events in Brazil). The work was intended to "activate" passive spectators to become "spect-actors" (a spectator who becomes active as an actor as well as an observer). Action and observation combine well for students too. Hence, Boal's "Image Theatre" has inspired me to adapt his methods to my needs in teaching religion.

One Boal exercise challenges participants to create sculptures in order to look at an issue first in the present, then past, and then future. Once the images are constructed, they are re-presented slowly (present, past, future) to show how the present image holds seeds of the past as well as the future within it. I have adapted this exercise to open the discussion of what is religious experience:

Sculptures in Past, Present, and Future

It's the second class session of my intro class (though it could also be the first). It's time to guide students into reflecting on their own religious experience. And so I begin the class with "I invite you to make a picture. We're going to use each others' bodies to do that. Let me explain.

We're going to split the class up into groups of four. You will have three people/bodies with which you will create a picture or sculpture. Think of their bodies as clay that you can mold. Because this course is called "Mystery and Meaning: An Introduction to Religious Studies" (I've also used this exercise in courses on mysticism, and biblical drama), I invite you to make three sculptures: one of your grandparents' experience of "mystery and meaning" (or religion, mysticism, Bible, etc), another of your parents' experience, and a third of your own experience. Some of you may want to choose your guardians, or a relative who raised you. Some of you may not have known your grandparents, but maybe you heard things about them and have an impression of them. Fine, use that to make a sculpture. Or perhaps you are only aware of your parents/guardian and yourself, not your grandparents. Fine, then do just two sculptures.

After each person creates two or three sculptures, take some group time to talk about the differences and similarities among all the sculptures you've experienced in your group. At the end of the process, after everyone in your group has had a chance to sculpt grandparents, parents or guardians, and self, then choose one person to show her three images to the whole class. You have thirty minutes to do this."

Student groups find a corner or go to other classrooms or outside. I walk around gauging the experience of the groups. While one group always thinks it is a race and finishes in five minutes, most groups take the time to discuss each of the sculptures and ask questions of one another. Thirty minutes later we are all reassembled. Each group has selected someone to show their sculptures to the class.

Sara's Sculptures (Group 1)

Past: We saw a Grant Wood–like depiction of a stern man and woman (as in Wood's *American Gothic*), each holding a book to the chest, while the opposite arm linked to the other spouse. Between the man's legs, a devil-like face with two fingers for horns poked its tongue out at us (see Figure 1).

Figure 1

Present: We saw a seated woman, bending over to hug a small upset child, played by another student (see Figure 2).

Figure 2

Future: We saw a young woman, seated cross-legged on the floor, breathing in and out, seemingly at peace in her solitude (see Figure 3).

Figure 3

Tom's Sculptures (Group 2)

Past (in two parts): We saw a man bending over in the act of planting, while two other students created another sculpture with movement—each slowly stood with their fingers moving near their faces. Later in the discussion we learned that each was a stalk of corn growing out of the earth.

Present (a sculpture with sound): We saw three people on their knees in a circle, holding hands, whispering softly. Later in the discussion we learned they were a family in daily prayer.

Future: We saw three students holding their arms out and up, close to one another, but separate. Later in the discussion we learned that they were "a cathedral of redwood trees."

After each series of sculptures, the presenting student/sculptor answers questions of clarification. Once all the groups have shown, we begin our inquiry into the nature of religious experience. I ask what these sculptures tell us about the experience of mystery and meaning. What do they tell us about different generations? We reflect on the importance of our past and present in shaping how we experience religions. The readings assigned for this session come from selections from autobiographies that chart spiritual journeys.

THEMATIC GROUP SCULPTURES

Sculpting can open a discussion of a particular topic or a broad idea, such as religion and violence, God, heaven, hell, afterlife, the Bible. The discussion of the topic follows the sculpting. Using this pedagogy, students enter a topic through their imaginations, creating with their bodies and with their peers.

At a biblical drama conference in Gelnhausen, Germany,[5] I used sculpting to address the suffering caused by and healing needed in biblical passages that deal with sexuality and spirituality. In two sessions, I engaged conference participants in creating living sculptures from biblical passages that have come to be called "clobber passages." These passages have historically been used to denigrate, batter, and maim anyone differing from current cultural norms. These passages include injunctions against homosexuality in Leviticus, passages from Paul that identify the subordinate place of women, and other passages that view the body and the flesh as sinful.

Each of ten groups of six people had a different clobber passage. They were directed to create two sculptures—one sculpture would express the existing clobber passage and use everyone in the group, and a second sculpture would express the rewritten version of the passage. I encouraged less discussion and more movement with the question "What does the feeling of that passage look like?" Three assumptions are operating in this question:

- discussion is the first and easiest way to enter into the passage, since most people need encouragement to begin engaging their bodies in the exploration;
- using the word "feeling" propels us past the cognitive into the experiential;
- our bodies respond more quickly to feelings than ideas, and are able to create vibrant images.

One group worked with 1 Corinthians 14: 33b–35, a passage in which women are admonished to keep silent and if they must learn, learn from their husbands. In this group there were four women pastors. These women recounted their painful struggles as women moving toward ordination and how their present congregations continue to question in a subtle way their knowledge and authority. The sculpture the group created had all the women in painful contortions, their mouths taped shut, with two male voices speaking the text menacingly. (This design had great resonance since the conference was held in Gelnhausen, a city that burned countless numbers of women during the Inquisition and to this day has preserved its own *Hexenturm*, or witches tower.)

Another group took the passage Leviticus 20:13, which states that if a man lies with another man, it is an abomination and both shall be put to death. Using Gary Comstock's research on the Book of Leviticus, this group examined the historical background of Leviticus, noting that it was compiled by returning Babylonian exiles to establish their exclusive privilege and power.[6] In rewriting the passage the group emphasized inclusivity. It became: when a woman lies with another woman, even the angels in heaven are made glad for eternity!

As each group shared the fruits of their explorations, it was palpably clear how painful these clobber passages were. As one participant said, "We have to live with this negativity in black and white." Another said "I'm trying with the old words of my religious socialization to try new things. When you find such clobber passages, I have learned to open them to life and joy." Tears and rage were threaded through each sculpture—from women and men. Rewriting and re-imaging the clobber passages were ways to begin to touch/feel the power of our own interpretations. Each passage became an opportunity to exorcize, empower, and enact.

Thematic Sculptures: The Exercise

It's important to model sculpting first. I ask a student to take any physical pose—but one that can be maintained for a period of time. After this, I physically connect with the student but in a different posture. If the student stood with arms stretched forward, I might stand back to back with him and stretch my arms forward, or I might face the student and take hold of both of her outstretched hands. The point is the physical connection with the other person (see Figure 4).

Figure 4

Figure 5

Create a circle with your students. Ask a volunteer to step to the center. Ask the student to respond physically to the theme (word or phrase you will say, e.g., family) and hold the pose (see Figure 5).

Invite other students to join the pose, one at time, physically connecting to someone in the sculpture. Each student joins with his own interpretation of the topic and connects to at least one other student in the sculpture. Together they create a still image/photograph/sculpture (see Figure 6).

Figure 6

An alternative sculpture that uses motion can also be created. The initial student starts with a gesture or movement that she can keep repeating. Students join with their own gesture/movements. When you use movement in sculptures, the sculpture appears to be machine-like. You can quicken the rhythm with side coaching, or slow it down.

You can feel when the sculpture is almost done. Sometimes there will be ten bodies engaged in it, sometimes as few as three. I always ask the students who watch, "Does this sculpture feel complete to you?"

Once the sculpture is complete, ask the students who are watching to walk all the way around it, to see facial expressions, body positions.

Ask one of the students on the periphery to give the sculpture a title. Other students may offer other titles.

Possible Follow-ups to Thematic Sculptures

If you want to keep mining the topic (and I always believe that the discussion is deeper if the students have been inspired and involved on several levels) try:

- Asking the students to sit and write their responses to the sculpture (s). You may want them to write in brief one-word-per-line responses or in narratives.
- Select a piece of music that might evoke the theme for you. Ask students to respond to the theme through movement/dance or through rhythm (what is the rhythm of God for you?) or ask the students to sketch (what is the shape of God for you?).

Discussion points:

- How do you see the theme reflected in the sculpture(s)?
- Is the title for the sculpture appropriate?
- What did you not see in the sculpture that is part of the theme?
- How does the sculpture relate to the reading assignment for this class?
- What did you learn about the topic from the sculpture(s) that you didn't know before?

ISSUE SCULPTURES

Making a three-dimensional interpretation, a sculpture, is a window into the mind and heart of the sculptor. When I begin our journey into Islam, I ask volunteers to create a series of sculptures of the Shahadah from the Qur'an, "There is no god but God, and Muhammad is the Messenger of God." Students have prepared for the class by reading selections from Coleman Bark's translations of Rumi's passionate poetry of the love between humans and the divine,[7] Frithjof Schuon's lyrical observations about Islam,[8] and selections from Akbar S. Ahmed's informative *Islam Today*.[9]

The first volunteer selects five students. He asks each student to lie on his/her back, in a circle, with arms and legs spread wide, and puts on his own face what he would like to see on the faces of the five. The expression is wide-eyed, with a slight open-mouthed smile. The sculptor student looks at his sculpture on the floor and sees it isn't quite what he thinks/feels. He then asks every other student in the sculpture to turn face down, still with arms and legs spread wide. He steps back and sighs, shaking his head up and down, pleased at what he sees. I ask him, "What is the title for your sculpture?" "God is everything" he says without hesitation. Indeed. I ask the class to remember this sculpture as we move on to others.

Another volunteer steps up. She selects one person and asks him to hold his hands to his heart and put his legs in a lunging position, with his head back, eyes gazing upward. "What is the title," I ask. A long pause, then she says softly, "Relationship."

Another student. She selects four students. She asks them to sit on the floor in different places in the classroom. Each is to sit with her/his hands clasped in their lap, gazing at a book on the floor with reverence. A title? "Everyday prayer."

Student Responses

The preceding work was created in response to the phrase: "There is no god but God, and Muhammad is the Messenger of God." Here are some student responses to the first sculpture, "God is everything":

- What I got was the circle. Like no beginning, no end.
- For me the people on their backs were looking at something really strongly like they were fascinated and the people on their stomachs were somehow part of it too.
- The people on their backs and on their stomachs were part of the same experience of God. Just different ways of showing it.
- I guess you could say it was all about unity. The circle included all kinds of people. But it felt like they were all one.
- The student who made the sculpture said that he was trying to show unity—that a Muslim seems to experience Allah in every aspect of his life, every thought and action. The people facing up were praying to Allah. The people facing down were praying too, showing honor to Allah. Nothing, he said, seemed to be outside the circle.

Here are responses to the second sculpture, "Relationship":

- I saw someone giving his heart.
- It was somebody who was giving his whole heart for something or somebody else.
- The student who made the sculpture said what had struck her from the reading was how Islam honored each individual's relationship with the divine.
- It felt like a very direct relationship, she said. Doing a sculpture of one person was also referring to Muhammad, she said, who must have had a very intense relationship with Allah as he received the Qur'an.

The following are responses to the third sculpture, "Everyday Prayer":

- I saw the importance of that book, the Qur'an.
- It was hard to see all of them, but the one who was sitting near me, I don't know, it felt like he was doing something he did every day.

- The student who made the sculpture said that she was trying to convey two things: one was that a person who sits on the floor reading the Qur'an seemed like a humble and holy person, and second, reading or reciting the Qur'an daily was a powerful everyday act for each person.

And with these remarks, we began our classroom discussion of the human-divine relationship in Islam.

Issue Sculpture: The Exercise

Model for the students with a volunteer how to create a sculpture. What you are modeling here is a respectful way of working with others' bodies to create your image/sculpture. Ask the volunteer to stand still, neutral, to be the clay from which you will fashion an image. Choose a word or phrase you are working with, for instance, belief, knowledge, learning. Then manipulate the arms, legs, or head, and so on, into a gesture (see Figure 7). I find that if I want someone to have a particular expression on his/her face, I put the expression on my face first and ask him/her to copy it. When students use this method they will most likely be working with more than one person in their sculpture.

Figure 7

Offer the students a word, sentence, phrase, or excerpt, i.e. belief. Ask them to close their eyes and visualize belief. Ask for a volunteer to create a sculpture, an image interpreting the word belief.

- The volunteer student selects a student and begins to physically manipulate that body to create the sculpture of belief, for example, placing a student on the floor (see Figure 8a).

Figure 8a

- The student selects other students to create the belief sculpture. Perhaps the student selects two other students and begins to place them on their backs, on the floor next to the first (see Figure 8b).

Figure 8b

- The student manipulates the limbs and faces of those in the sculpture to reflect his interpretation of belief; perhaps the student has selected five students and now arranges the five bodies, moving their arms and legs wide (see Figure 8c).

Note: Be sure to have the student create the sculpture in a place in the classroom that all can see.

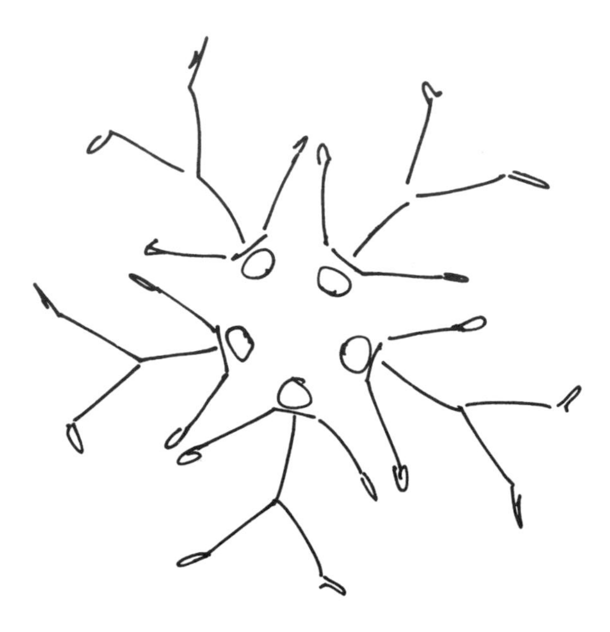

Figure 8c

Possible side coaching for the teacher while the student creates the sculpture:

- Try to create the sculpture with as little talking as possible—concentrate on the physical image you are creating.
- Don't leave out the face and what expression you want on it.
- Where are the eyes of each person in the sculpture focused?
- If you want a particular feeling in a body you are working with, show the person by doing it yourself first and let her or him copy you.

Once the student is finished creating the sculpture, you may wish to ask him to title it as a way to further explore his interpretation of the original word, phrase, or text.

Ask the rest of the class what they see. Encourage students in their comments to say first what they see, and second, what the sculpture makes them feel.

Depending on your leaning toward technology, you may want to take a picture of each sculpture and at a later date when you are concluding that section of the course, show them. This may help students recall their first impressions of the topic. Or you may want to create new sculptures and compare them to the earlier images.

OTHER TECHNIQUES FOR BEGINNING DISCUSSIONS

Sculptures into Scenes

Often a sculpture that is created by the class can be the inspiration for both characters and scenes. For example, if a "Kaddish" sculpture had people in it whose body postures suggested characters such as "God" and "human," you could create an improvised scene between these two characters. In the next chapter we will define and give examples of what characters and improvisations are, and how to create them.

Interview Techniques

In my introductory class in religion, sometime in the first three weeks we look at definitions of religion and spirituality from practitioners in the town that surrounds the university. I ask three or four students to interview ministers, priests, or spiritual teachers whom I have previously contacted. The students are each given a specific question to begin the conversation. The student's goal is to listen actively and in the next class session "become" the person interviewed by saying his/her exact words and taking on his/her gestures. I will say more about this technique in chapter 5.

In the same course, as I begin each section on Hinduism, Buddhism, Judaism, Christianity, and Islam, I also use the interview technique but in a slightly different format. I ask all the students in the class to interview two people they don't know about Buddhism, for example. They ask "What is Buddhism?" The students are to return to class and "become" the people they interviewed. In chapter 5, I will say much more about this technique of interviewing as well as the stereotypes that we invariably encounter. Suffice it to say here that through this exercise we face and dissect stereotypes through the ensuing discussion.

Word Pools

On beginning a new topic, I will often use the technique of "word pools." This technique builds on students' initial impressions of a topic from their reading or from their experience. For example, early on in the course, I take two words, "religion" and "spirituality," and ask students to say out loud any word associations they may have.

This is a good exercise to use after warm-ups when students are loose and their minds are open. I often have them lie on their backs and offer free associations from this very relaxed position. Examples I have received include:

- *Religion:* Doctrines for behavior, organized framework for spirituality, catalyst for historical events, beliefs, worship, individual religious practices, faith, how you were brought up, a group that looks at things the same way, guidance, rituals
- *Spirituality:* Daily practices, an understanding of motivation and driving forces in life, a higher power, individual interpretation, changeable

From this word pool several different possibilities present themselves.

- A lecture and discussion about "religion" and "spirituality" and their differences can begin.
- Sculptures can be made of "religion" and "spirituality" to take the word pool into a nonverbal and three-dimensional realm.
- A brief writing exercise can ask students to reflect on the words generated. Afterwards you may want to ask for volunteers to read their work.

CONCLUSION

What makes people enter into conversation, become drawn into the stream of thoughts, feel safe enough to express their opinions? Beginning discussions, no matter the topic, is an art. It should be no surprise then that art, in this case theatre, offers new methods for doing just that.

When discussions become stalled, it is often due to individuals withdrawing from the conversation because they devalue their own ideas. Just as an instructor attempts to teach/lecture in different modalities for different kinds of learners, so students need new models and methods for finding their own voices and ideas. The techniques of sculpting offered here in chapter 3 are designed to give students a sense of their own unique contribution to discussing a topic. At the same time, the inventive particularity of others' embodied ideas is appreciated. When creation stories are enacted or sculptures embodied, students witness one another thinking, playing, and imagining with their bodies. On each of those levels, students experience their own and others' unique contributions.

But what are the implications for the use of this pedagogy? Students learn that ideas can be imaged and enfleshed. Whether a student entrusts his or her body to another, or discovers the mutuality of creating images with the bodies of peers, the message is that learning can be collaborative. Scholarship and imagination are partners. And what of the implications for religious studies and theology lurking behind the sculptures in this chapter? The Holy has been glimpsed by men and women of all religions. Those visions interpret the ineffable. Beliefs, values, and God-talk must find expression within our imaginations and find form in our lives. The classroom is a place to dream and rehearse both enduring and new visions.

4

improvisation in the classroom

I RECALL A YOUNG ACTRESS in my intermediate acting class at the American Conservatory Theatre. We were doing an improvisation exercise called "Who am I?" She was to make an entrance into a space where another actor would greet her and begin a conversation with her. The goal for the actress was to guess her relationship to the other actor, based solely on the improvised dialogue between them, and create a character based on that guess. From the moment she came into the space, we all saw that she had a preconceived notion of who her character was. She stood with her back against the wall smiling at him. When he said it was good to see her, she slinked over to him, put her arms around his neck and purred. He backed away, embarrassed. "I don't think that's supposed to happen," he said. She advanced on him, continuing to purr, "Baby, don't be shy with me, please, baby."

I stopped the exercise. "Teresa," I said, "What kind of roles do you usually play when you are cast in a play?"

"Well," she said laughing, "usually they're kind of bimbos, you know sexy women with no brains."

"Aaaah," I said. "It seems to me that you have played that role so often that, given the chance to do something else, you revert to the 'bimbo.' You've been cast in bimbo roles over and over again, and so you think it's the only thing you can do as an actress."

Teresa laughed and offered, "I never thought of it that way."

When we began the exercise again, I coached from the sidelines. The actor created a new relationship for Teresa to guess. She entered and he said, "Hell, I thought you would never get here!"

I coached, "Listen to him, really hear him, try not to prejudge what he's offering you."

"If you don't do something fast . . ." he said looking squarely at something he saw near him.

She looked at him, unsure of herself. "I'm sorry I was late."

"Okay, okay, just do something, please," he gestured her toward him.

She hesitated again, this time watching him closely, noting his gaze and gestures. "Well . . . I'll need someone to help me get scrubbed for the operation" she said.

"Right, doc, I'm with you."

"Okay then, here we go." Teresa pantomimed washing her hands and then held them up for the actor to place gloves on them. She sighed and stepped toward the operating room. "Scalpel" she said firmly, putting out her hand. Teresa listened, observed, touched, and therefore engaged with what was presented to her. As she stepped into the reality of the improvisation, a new reality in herself opened up. She was leaving the bimbo behind.

Improvisation begins with a positive position—saying "yes" to whatever happens.

In each moment, the improviser takes what is offered to her, adds to it, integrates it, and then gives it back to the other so that something new can happen. Spontaneity is the moment when we are "freed to relate and act, involving ourselves in the moving, changing world around us."[1] The underlying principle of improvisation is that each person in the exercise is listening and responding to the other—in the present moment and with the whole body. In a way, improvisation is a state of mind. In fact, it has a lot to do with Buddhism. Every moment calls forth awareness and also becomes an opportunity.

> Before we can play (experience), we must be free to do so. It is necessary to become part of the world around us and make it real by touching it, seeing it, feeling it, tasting it, and smelling it—direct contact with the environment is what we seek. It must be investigated, questioned, accepted or rejected. The personal freedom to do so leads us to experiencing and thus to self-awareness (self-identity) and self expression. The hunger for self-identity and self-expression, while basic to all of us, is also necessary for theatre expression.[2]

In theatre, improvisation is a game in which players set about working with a specific frame, structure, and goal. The player lives in the present moment filled with her own impulses and those of others. In the present moment we are freed from handed-down frames of reference (roles such as bimbos), memories filled with judgments or hearsays. The player is asked to respond to a person in an environment—to see, hear, explore and then speak and act accordingly. Inside the game/exercise, the player offers herself and receives multiple stimuli from other players.

In improvisation we can experience bits and pieces of ourselves. It is a time of discovery, meeting new parts of ourselves that are called out by the improvisation. This method is also an opportunity to rehearse how we would like to be in our ever changing world—aware of our environments, exploring life as an adventure, meeting each situation without judgment and without fear.

Improvisation can be applied to different types of courses. In a biblical drama course, I use improvisation to deepen students' experience of the texts that we study. The class is an introductory course to biblical studies and religious studies. Its objectives are to acquaint students with biblical literature/biblical studies, and introduce them to new pedagogical methods such as dramatic writing and the development and enactment of characters. Students study exegesis and midrash when reading scripture passages, including feminist and womanist approaches. Improvisation is used to elicit students' interpretations of texts and to prepare them for writing contemporary scenes that parallel the biblical stories studied.

When we take up the Abrahamic cycle in the Hebrew Bible, we look closely at the stories of Sarah and Hagar, the mothers of the Jewish and Arab races. Their relationship, as seen in Genesis, appears to be one of jealousy and abuse. Midrash also reflects this. As further background we read suras regarding Ishmael and Ibrahim from the Qur'an and its commentaries. Students encounter Hagar's journey through the scholarship of Phyllis Trible, Delores Williams, Barbara Freyer Stowasser and Renita Weems. They read of the many faces of Hagar depicted by these and other writers. She is presented as a symbol of oppression, her story as one of survival, not liberation. Beyond racial and ethnic differences with Sarah, the two women can be seen for what they had in common under patriarchy. With this research, the Genesis depiction of Sarah and Hagar takes on further complexity. Students witness the variance in interpretations. But the freedom to interpret, to create midrash, also needs to be experienced. We do this through improvisation.

BUILDING A CHARACTER: MOVEMENT IMPROVISATION

Our bodies know. Consciously and unconsciously, we take into our bodies all that we come in contact with. Our bodies hold our experience. For this reason alone, allowing our entire body to express feelings and responses is healthy. Inviting the spine, the legs, the head, the arms, and the torso to express helps to unblock and balance. Thus, when we begin to explore a character, I turn first to the body to express its knowledge

In my biblical drama class, we spend three to four weeks on each story. In the second and third weeks, once the students have read the biblical passages, exegesis, midrash, and commentaries, we begin to improvise with movement.

Movement Improvisation: The Exercise

To each student, I pass out two sheets of paper and provide markers. I play music to put a different frame around our work together. I ask students to draw (abstractly or realistically), the faces of Sarah and Hagar (one face per sheet of paper). Then I ask them to make holes for eyes to create a mask; sometimes we use rubber bands poked through holes on the side of the mask to help hold the mask on our heads (if you have the budget to buy "neutral masks" for everyone, then students can paint them in the same interpretive manner). Working with a mask gives students a margin of freedom to explore body expression. When the face is hidden, the body is freed. To put it another way, the mask forces the body to communicate. Thus masks reveal rather than conceal. The body communicates character. The way a head bends or arms and legs move will signify a different energy/person/persona. Once the masks are completed, we push back the desks to make an open space.

The students choose one of their masks, and begin to move about the room with the music. They explore the characters of Hagar and Sarah through movement and rhythm. This improvisation allows the body and mind to integrate the reading and discussions.

Coaching: Use your entire body to express Sarah or Hagar—from hands to feet! Explore new choices, don't get stuck in your first reaction to a character.

Once I begin to see the emergence of a character in students' movements, I ask them to begin to approach another person in the room, but without words. Nothing is written on their masks, so the only way students know which character is approaching is by paying attention to the movements. What happens when a Hagar meets another Hagar or a Sarah?

When I clap, students move to another partner, discover who they are and begin a new improvisation. Because each partner offers different stimuli, each coupling becomes an opportunity to explore new aspects of a character.

Once the exercise is underway, I add, "use sound (not words) as well as movement to interact." We hear grunts, moans, sighs, whimpering, laughter. The combination of sound and movement further energizes the players.

Though we are exploring two female characters, the men in the class don't feel left out. They too have made masks and I coach them to "find the Sarah in you or the Hagar in you!" Doing cross-gender work is always a challenge. When it works, male students discover new physicalities (even if they are stereotypes). All of it is good for discussion afterward. (For example, how does patriarchy enshrine gender roles, and to what purpose? What are the parallels between the gender roles in the biblical story and today?)

Before discussion begins, I follow the movement improvisation with a "free writing exercise" in which students reflect on 1) "becoming" Hagar or Sarah, and 2) the movement improvisation with their various partners.

Student Responses:

- I thought Sarah was "white bread." I didn't know she had so many parts, so many different ways of playing Sarah.
- I often compare myself to others who are more physically fluid and quick in body movements and rhythm. However, I stayed with it and did my own style!
- The integration of body, mind, and heart really happened for me. The readings about Sarah and Hagar were stimulating, and using

improvisation helped me integrate insights with my own experiences and truly embody them!

- I learned that my body is a source of wisdom. I also found that the wealth there is in scripture can be plumbed by mediating it through the body.

•

Even though in the beginning the movements and interactions of students may be self-conscious, with the help of the masks, the students will gradually allow themselves to play and interact with others. When they work without words, learning to depend on the ability of their bodies to integrate what they know, students find a personal feeling/understanding/knowledge for each biblical character.

Movement improvisation brought us this far. Building on this personal connection to a character, we begin a new exercise, the interview.

Building a Character: The Interview

I ask for a volunteer to be interviewed as Sarah or Hagar (students can work with their mask or without it in this exercise). The person sits on "the hot seat" to face her or his audience. I welcome Sarah or Hagar to "The Babba Wawa Show (Barbara Walters)."

The student, in character, answers questions, improvising the responses. Though the answers are created in the moment, I encourage students in their responses to integrate knowledge from class readings as well as their own intuitive knowledge of the character.

In the interview I ask questions and encourage other class members to do the same. The impetus for the questions comes from Konstantin Stanislavski's method for creating a character.[3] These are some of the questions asked:

- Tell us about your childhood (Hagar or Sarah). Where did you grow up? Tell us about your family.

- When you were growing up, what future did you see for yourself?
- How did you first meet Abraham?
- How did you first meet Sarah (or Hagar)?
- Do you have a good friend? Describe that person.
- How would you describe your relationship to Abraham? To Sarah? To Hagar?
- What are your best personality traits?
- What's a recent dream that you have had? How would you describe the times in which you live? Politically? Economically? Religiously?
- What do you want for your life? For your child?
- What are the obstacles in the way of getting what you want?
- What do you do (your actions) to get what you want?
- Have you ever had a near death experience?
- What's your relationship with God/Yahweh/Ra?

Why do all this? Why do an interview and create a character through improvisation?

Through readings, the student encounters with his mind/body a text and interpretations of that text. But the content is only partially understood. This exercise builds on the movement improvisation and makes the student's process whole with enacted knowledge. Becoming a character, the student enters into his own spontaneous interpretation. This interpretation of the character is in fact a blend of himself, the biblical text, and the readings.

The improvised Hagar sighs, gestures, finds words, scratches her head. She experiences uncertainty, speaks of injustice, is shy, perhaps expresses anger, feels conflict. The character has many variables and nuances. The student discovers something larger than herself, an amalgam, in fact, of herself and another. This is the character who ceases to be an ancient removed entity and becomes a fascinating persona. Hagar/Sarah lives now, and through her we hear of urgent conflicts of justice, theophanies, cruelty, friendship, motherhood.

The techniques of movement and interview can be used to enact a character in a story or an idea, such as compassion in the study of Buddhism (imagine drawing a mask of compassion, students moving to music embodying compassion, being interviewed as "compassion"). However you choose to use this work, it is an opportunity for play, imagination, integration. However, the students must feel that what they say will not be judged as inappropriate or silly or wrong. Spontaneity succeeds or fails on the safety of the process.

SCENE IMPROVISATION BASED ON A TEXT

This section invites you to create an improvisational experience that will not only allow your class to enter more thoroughly into a story or an idea, but also teach students to observe, to be aware of our behaviors as human beings. For that is the end result of looking at Abraham, Sarah, Hagar, and others—to behold our own humanity in our search for meaning.

In my teaching I use scene improvisation to create connection between students and material. In my biblical drama class, as we continue to work with the Abrahamic cycle, I ask students to improvise the story, in their own words. Now the mask is off. Now it is you and the other, face to face.

There are key methods to every scene improvisation. The shorthand formula is who, where, when, and what. Before an improvisation begins, each character in the scene needs to know: Who am I? Where am I? When is it? What is the situation?

Who am I?

The story that began this chapter depicted a "Who am I?" exercise. It is an initial step toward teaching students to develop a character with their whole bodies, in addition to spoken words. The movement and then the interview improvisations described earlier are also exercises to answer the question "Who am I?"[4]

Where am I? When is it?

Each scene takes place in a specific where. By "where" I mean the place, but also the time. In its physicalization, or physical expression, theatre is all about creating a story in time and space. There are theatre games that are fun to introduce this idea to your students. One simple exercise begins with one student creating a where (and a time) without words, and others joining when they guess the environment being offered. For example, one student begins actions for pitching a tent at dusk when s/he can barely see. When students think they know the where and when being offered, they whisper to the teacher. If they are correct, the teacher waves them into joining the where and when. Students might join the environment with making a fire, unrolling sleeping bags, helping to pitch the tent, and so on. The point is for everyone in the exercise to create specific actions/movements in relationship to their environment.[5]

If we applied "Where am I?" to an improvisation with Sarah and Hagar, it might look like this: It is mid-afternoon in Hagar's tent, or it is mid-afternoon in Sarah's tent.

What is the situation?

This question covers the context and characters for the improvisation. It is important that this include what each character wants, what his or her intention is. The following is an example of setting up the situation for an improvisation with Hagar and Sarah.

- Hagar has been taking care of little Ishmael all day. It is mid-afternoon. Ishmael is finally down for a nap in Sarah's tent. Hagar wants to take advantage of this rest time for herself too and lies down near him.
- Sarah enters in a huff because Abraham has just asked her to prepare a big meal for a group of surprise visitors and she wants Hagar's help, or she wants Hagar to do it.
- You have set up the situation and now each character knows what she wants both for herself and from the other. Hagar wants to rest

and to be left in peace to do so. Sarah wants help from Hagar to comply with Abraham's inconvenient request (or she wants Hagar to deal with it entirely).

- The improvisation will reveal what each woman does to get what she wants.
- Improvisations can last a couple of minutes, or five minutes. The length is up to you. You will feel when the scene has run its course.

The who, where, when, and what are complete. The improvisation can now begin. We have created the set-up. We know that there are two characters in this scene: Sarah and Hagar (plus baby Ishmael). We know that it is mid-afternoon and Hagar is lying next to Ishmael in Sarah's tent to take a nap. Sarah enters flustered with Abraham's last-minute request for a meal for unexpected guests. Students now have a framework in which to play. They have characters, a time, and place, and they have an intention.

An Improvisation

The following scene was an improv that two women students did, given the above information of who, what, when, where:

SARAH (talking to herself as she enters the tent): Every blessed time. Every stranger that passes by. Famous for his generosity—right! When you don't have to cook, Mr. Abraham, it's easy!

HAGAR (wakes up with the noise): Shhhh. (She motions Sarah to be quiet because Ishmael is asleep.)

SARAH: Okay, Okay (she draws Hagar to a corner and whispers). Dearest (running her hands through Hagar's hair). I know I've asked more of you in the last week than anyone has a right to.

HAGAR (whispering): Sarah, I'm doing my best with your husband. But he's just so old. It's very difficult.

SARAH (whispering): Believe me—I know what you are talking about. (They giggle quietly.) But it will happen, I really do believe it will. I'm just so grateful . . .

HAGAR (making a face): Is there some herb or stimulant you could give him? (They both laugh again.)

SARAH: I love Abraham . . . but sometimes! Oh God! I almost forgot. Guests! I can't do it in time, sweetheart. It's Abraham's thing . . . you know, another impromptu feast for strangers.

HAGAR: And you need my wizardry.

SARAH: Yes.

HAGAR: Under one condition.

SARAH: What's that?

HAGAR: You sleep with him tonight.

SARAH: Oh my God . . . (laughs) Yes . . . anything . . . I'll do it.

HAGAR: Deal.

The two women students, not knowing what the outcome would be, had to listen carefully to one another. Key to their improv was the spirit of give and take; neither had all the answers. They depended on each other for the scene to evolve. They also depended on the improvisation framework supplied beforehand of who, where, when, and what. When teachers carefully lead their students through physicalizations of a character, interviews, and then provide a framework (the process followed in this chapter), improvisations become occasions for building confidence. The two women students who created this improv effectively communicated with each other. For women students, in particular, finding their voices can be a public and a personal act of courage and empowerment. Theatre offers this challenge and opportunity in your classroom.

The improvised scene above reflects questions raised by the class readings such as: Do we have to accept the jealousy depicted in the biblical text between these two women? What was the relationship of these two women? The two students were willing to reimagine Sarah and Hagar. I encourage students in these improvs to blend issues that have intrigued them from the class readings with their own contemporary experience. That's what you hear in their words. That is the spirit of using improvisation in the classroom.

The discussion that followed this scene was heated. Was this type of relationship really possible in patriarchal times? Could women be friends in this situation? How is power negotiated by these women from their different positions? Could women find ways to subvert patriarchal power? What is the redactor of the text trying to say through the relationship depicted in Genesis? What do you understand from this scene that is timeless? The gender of the discussants was sometimes a factor in the positions taken. That was noted. The improvisation had been played by two white women students. Could this same scene have been played by a white and a black woman? Was the relationship depicted possible between women of different races? What is the role of race in the Genesis story?

Through improvisation, characters and their situations take on depth, complexity, humanity. Your students are challenged to identify with the characters and by so doing discover empathy. Empathy creates a bridge to the other, to the material of your course, to one another.

REWRITING THE TEXT

A further step I offer to students in my biblical drama class is to take a biblical story and bring it into the twenty-first century through either improvised or written work. In years past I have seen:

- Genesis 13 and 19: the story of Lot and his family depicted as Mrs. Lot struggles to open up the restrictions of a gated community
- Genesis 19: 1–29: Mrs. Lot in a police station reporting a crime in which she was mugged from behind with the threat "Don't turn around!"
- Genesis 16, 17, 21:1–21: the story of Sarah, Abraham, and Hagar, transformed into childless Sarah and Abe making the decision to use a surrogate mother; also witnessed as Sarah and Hagar struggling to create a friendship, one being the adoptive mother and the other the biological mother

- Book of Ruth: the story of Ruth and Naomi seen as the story of Naomi in a senior home visited daily by Ruth

Bringing biblical stories into the present assists students in experiencing the relevance of biblical literature and seeing its links to social justice issues. Students also witness why these stories have survived in religious traditions. They experience multiple perspectives on a story. They come to understand the value of midrash.

CONCLUSION

Improvisation provides forms in which students feel safe to explore new ideas and new ways of expressing themselves. Creating characters and improvisations offers students a new level of confidence. One student said to me "I can see parts of myself in all the female biblical characters we studied." Yes, and there is also the possibility of discovering new parts of yourself! Learning to let go, to feel the liquid fluidity of an improvisation, knowing that you are not in charge, is indeed a leap of faith. One student called it "pushing the level of my comfort zones." Surprises are plentiful!

An improvisation can be created by individuals, couples, or groups. The key dynamic of the improvisation is give and take, ebb and flow, surrender and action. In this respect, improv teaches students the value of cooperation. Students also discover new ideas and feelings in themselves and with others. The interior experience of doing an improvisation is very much akin to the state we knew as children called play. When we allow ourselves to physically enter into the creation of story, becoming the characters, we join intelligence, articulation, intuition, and imagination. Said better, it integrates body, mind, and spirit.

Two students in a recent biblical drama course voice two different results of improvisation. Embodiment and enactment can propel us out of assumptions and bring us face to face with real feelings; in improvisation we take on physicalities and characters that can bring us to new empathies with "the other."

I brought to this study of Hagar, Sarai, and Abram very particular and somewhat rigid ideas about the characters and the "rights" that certain ones had to speak to me. I am the African American granddaughter of sharecroppers and the great-granddaughter of slaves and, as such, was closed to the voices of Abram and Sarai while extremely supportive of Hagar's voice. Reading many of the required documents prior to class and being steeped in some years of the black church reading of the account, I was fueled by a righteous indignation over Hagar's seeming lack of power and place. Had this been purely a lecture class, I am not confident that I would have witnessed a change in my attitude. At the intellectual level it is often too easy to defend against any uneasiness bubbling up in one's body and spirit. When that body and spirit, however, become the primary vehicle through which knowledge is imparted, superceding the intellect, it is nearly impossible to deny that insight which comes, in fact, from the human core. Not only did this study force me to reach out to Sarai and Abram, it invited me to bring Hagar down from the pedestal on which I had placed her and to meet her on the human plane with all its potential for pettiness and greatness.[6]

By enfleshing the biblical story, its meaning changes from cognitive to corporeal. I remember walking around the room, trying to walk like Ishmael. I had my chest pushed out, I walked with a strut, and I stuck my jaw up and high, as if to domineer. Now, my body remembers the experience of Ishmael, not just words or images associated with his name. My body also remembers the experience of being YHWH, who accompanies Hagar after she first ran away. I remember bending over and pretending I had terrible stomach pain, which represented all the pain that she too experienced. I intended to show God suffering as we do. I remember now a fullness to that feeling as I think of God as a co-sufferer.[7]

5

toward a theology of memorization and enactment

> In a city in Saudi Arabia, a boy who is auspiciously four years, four months, and four days old, celebrates a special event. He goes to school to recite officially his first verse of the Qur'an. The verse is written in honey on a small slate. He recites it formally and the honey is dissolved in water. The boy then drinks the water that has been sweetened by the holy words of the Qur'an. The words he has spoken now become a part of him, and he returns home with his family to a celebration.[1]

MEMORIZATION AND RECITATION OF SACRED TEXTS are important practices for experiencing the world's religions. The words of scriptures spoken, chanted, and recited through the centuries seem to contain a power of their own. When spoken, can they unlock an experience of the Divine? In my teaching, this is the question. When students take sacred texts inside them through memorization, is it possible that they can, for a moment, touch in themselves some essence of the Divine? Is it possible that they can, for a moment, enter into the religious experience of the faith we are studying?

Memory is the loam of the present. From this earth, the present blossoms. In every religious tradition, origins are preserved through memory. Religions preserve their beginnings through memorized stories and teachings of their founders passed down through generations. Memory also marks time. Calendars offer a quilt of religious feast days, holidays, sacred time. Each year is sacralized through memory. We recall the past to enrich and sanctify the present. Religious ritual is enacted memory that calls the past into the present and in so doing transforms it.

Sacred texts are often memorized. "Qur'an" means recitation. The children of the poor learn Arabic through memorizing and reciting the Qur'an in madrasas (Islamic religious schools). A fragment of the Torah is tied to the forehead and the arm (phylacteries), viscerally binding it to one's memory and body. The *Mahabarahata* is memorized and enacted by school children each year at Mt. Madonna School in Watsonville, California. The Bhagavad-Gita is recited by a holy man; those that listen in true faith know that they will win release from suffering and rebirth. At the beginning of their training, Buddhist monks and nuns memorize The *Dhammapada* (Path of Teaching). On a lighter note, having grown up in Catholic grammar schools, I can still recite many of the questions and answers from the Baltimore Catechism!

The use of memorization and enactment of sacred texts asks students to encounter themselves, perhaps in a new ways. In memorizing texts and enactments, students are involved in somatic learning using body, thought, and feeling. With its emphasis on religious experience, this approach demands that a teacher make herself available for students. With free writing exercises, reflection papers, and conversations during office hours, students have the opportunity for conversation about their class work. Throughout my years of teaching, I have never encountered a student who feared to memorize a text because it might change him or her, or introduce a new feeling. But that moment is certainly possible. This is why one-on-one conversations and building an environment of trust is so important. I have, however, certainly encountered students who were nervous or fearful about memorization. In those moments, I use my intuition of that student. If I can see that a student is upset and made more nervous by not holding (literally) the text they have memorized, I will say, "Fine, if that helps you relax," or even, "Please, refer to it if you need it." If, however, I intuit that a student can recite without reference to a text, but won't allow himself or herself to do that, then I insist on the student at least attempting it. The point is for each student to experience the text in a new way because he or she has taken it inside and thus speaks aloud the words from his or her inner landscape to the rest of the class. In chapter 8 I will say more about a student's experience of fear and emotion.

MEMORIZATION OF RELIGIOUS TEXTS

It was the third week of the Intro to Religious Studies course. By now students knew to expect "the weird." The following week, we were to begin our study of Hinduism. In spite of their expectations, students still sat amazed as I went around the room pointing to each and making the assignment. "Joe, stanza 1. Todd, stanza 2, Mary, stanza 3 . . ." and so on. I assigned every verse, in succession, from the second book of the Bhagavad Gita or Song of God for the students to memorize. This meant going around the room three times. Mouths dropped open. The second book develops the dialogue between Arjuna and Krishna and sets out major themes about the nature of the self and one's duty that the following sixteen books amplify.

Next, I moved to the twelfth book of the Gita. An audible shock wave was heard and a slow sigh of relief as students realized it was "only twenty" verses. Once again I assigned each verse in succession to memorize. The twelfth book speaks of the results of this theophany, the revelation of the divine.

All in all, each student had received four stanzas. If the exercise worked, the entire text of books two and twelve of the Bhagavad Gita would be recited and heard in next week's class.

The following week found us sitting in a large circle on the floor and doing prajna breathing (see chapter 2). It helped calm and focus everyone since they had arrived fidgety and a bit nervous. With that we began the recitation of books two and twelve. The profound poetry of the Gita slowly took on life with each student's voice.

Student #1 in a quiet voice spoke Sanjaya's opening lines:

Arjuna sat dejected,
filled with pity,
his sad eyes blurred by tears.
Krishna gave him counsel.

Student #13 looked at the entire circle and spoke directly to us as Krishna:

Never have I not existed,
nor you, nor these kings;
and never in the future
shall we cease to exist.

Student #27 stared at the floor for the words of Krishna:

When one gives up desires in his mind,
is content with the self within herself,
then one is said to be a person
whose insight is sure, Arjuna.

Student # 1 smiled knowingly and spoke Krishna's words:

Neutral to blame and praise,
silent, content with his fate,
unsheltered, firm in thought,
the person of devotion is dear to me.[2]

The ideas and images of the Gita swirled around the circle again and again. Some spoke softly, some looked up, some stared at their hands or feet searching for an elusive word (two had even written verses on their hands and arms), some spoke clearly and looked around the circle as they spoke. I offered words or phrases from the text to students who needed help.

The Song of God, a conversation between Arjuna and Krishna, had occurred with multiple student voices. For a moment, we were all Arjuna and Krishna. Though each student had spent time taking the Gita's words inside them, now in the circle, individual stanzas took on meaning within the web of the whole. Words memorized in isolation from the whole became part of a living, breathing story. How did I know this? I could hear meaning take shape in student's voices. In the beginning, voices recited the stanzas in monotone recitation. But as each stanza was followed by the next, the linkage created a web of the whole breathing story: voices became melodic and rhythmic, pauses were organic, word emphasis came from understanding. When I heard the highs and lows of students' voices, heard confidence, even interpretation, I knew they had made contact with meaning. They were experiencing meaning.

When we were done, we sat in silence, taking in the enormity of what we had just accomplished. And yes, there were sighs of relief too!

Student Responses

- Memorizing sections of the Gita made me realize that memorizing is something one does every day . . . although difficult, memorizing the lines does make them become part of you. With every word spoken in the stanzas I memorized, I felt them in my heart. I also envisioned them in my own way. What I memorized becomes like a dream filled with words and visions . . . once memorized well enough, the dream becomes a reality, I have become part of those lines.

- When I memorized the sections of the Gita they became a part of my mind and it is because of this that they almost became a part of me. In situations where they were relevant (however slight), parts of them would enter my thought processes, sometimes lingering on for minutes at a time, sometimes so fleeting that I would hardly recognize them.

- I had a hard time memorizing my stanzas from the Gita because it was only a small part that, when read by itself, didn't mean anything. But when we sat down and all the stanzas got spoken, my stanzas came alive with the others.

•

Later, I asked the students to write on the board in words or phrases the themes of book two and twelve. From these, we chose one—attachment. With discussion, we settled on the strong parallel between addiction and attachment. Then I invited the students to create a sound/gesture sculpture about it. One student began with a crouch and a sucking sound of smoking marijuana. Seven other students joined in. They brought gestures of drinking and drunkenness, someone sleeping away her college years, someone with a mouthful of chocolates, even addiction to sex was offered with a gesture and a hungry leer. When we felt the sculpture was finished, we walked around this group of interwoven bodies, noting details, facial expressions—the leering received a lot of attention! Then, with the sculpture still in place, I asked students to title it using words and phrases they had memorized from the Gita. Several sculpture titles were offered: "There is nothing else!" "Obsessed with powers and delights!" "From attachment desire arises." "Without peace, where is his joy?"

Next, I asked for a volunteer to reshape the people in the sculpture into a new one that reflected the opposite—impartiality. The student created a circle of people, seated on the floor, with their backs to one another, looking out at us, sitting in lotus positions (as best they could), breathing. Again we all walked around the sculpture, looking for details. Again I asked for titles from the Gita text for the sculpture: "He does not rejoice or hate, grieve or feel desire . . ."; "One who bears hate for no creature"; "Action without craving"; "Peace." In the discussion that followed, other students described how they would offer different images of impartiality. One person in a lotus position, he suggested, or a person with a butterfly perched on his shoulder—beholding its beauty without disturbing it. Our discussion branched out into other Gita themes as well as reflections on the group recitation and sculpture exercise.

MEMORIZATION OF RELIGIOUS TEXTS AND ENACTMENT

The scene shifts; the methods remain similar. We are beginning the section on Buddhism. After reading *Being Peace,* by Thich Nhat Hanh, I introduce *vipassana*, or mindfulness meditation, as an aspect of religious experience. As an experience of mindfulness, students have been instructed to memorize a "gatha" written by Thich Nhat Hanh. "Gathas" are small poems that when repeated with everyday actions usher in an awareness of the present moment and our connectedness to other human beings. Just as Judaism blesses every day acts such as waking, bathing, and eating with a prayer, so the text of gathas makes us conscious of our individual actions and their ability to be transformative moments for ourselves and our world.

Serving food:

In this food,
I see clearly the presence
of the entire universe
supporting my existence.[3]

Brushing your teeth:

Brushing my teeth and rinsing my mouth,
I vow to speak purely and lovingly.
When my mouth is fragrant with right speech,
a flower blooms in the garden of my heart.[4]

Memorization and enactment are not just reciting the lines. Students memorize a gatha and are asked in class to "enact" the gatha, such as brushing your teeth. In front of the class, the student does the physical action that the gatha describes. It is a full body commitment to the interpretation of the memorized words. Once the words are inside you, they guide and sing the body. Each gatha causes consciousness to be wed to simple daily actions. They are crystallized examples of contained physical moments (brushing your teeth, sweeping the floor, taking out the garbage, looking at your toes or hand, opening a window). Presenting in front of a class can be uncomfortable. Concentrating on the simplicity of the physical actions referenced in each gatha assists the student in letting go of performing. In enacting the gatha, the student does a familiar action from daily life. This familiarity combined with the brevity of the gatha text allows the student to more easily experience the power of word and action. But enacting gathas should not be wooden recitations. Students need to be encouraged to commit their full energies to embodying the words, and to being totally present by breathing throughout the action. The gatha, spoken aloud with the action, carves out the specificity of the physicalization. Students experience the wholeness of word and action. This is embodiment.

It is the dance of text and action that the body remembers. Not only are the gathas easier to memorize when combined with action, but the student will also be able to recall his or her gatha weeks later because words/meaning are coupled with physical action. This is the somatics of memory.

I also use these gathas in a course "Enacting Mysticism" because they reveal the oneness of all life. In that course, a woman student had chosen the gatha for washing feet and offered to share it with us in class. "Peace and joy in each toe—my own peace and joy."[5] She sat on the floor, took her shoes and socks off, and began to heartily rub the toes of her feet. Breathing steadily, fully engaged with the sight of her toes, she repeated her gatha over and over again. She began to cry, still focusing on her toes. And slowly she began to laugh. All the while, the words of the gatha floated like water lilies over her sea of emotions. The entire class seemed to sigh in recognition of her toes/our toes. Afterwards she told us that her feet, particularly her toes, had been broken, sprained, and cut many times in her life. During the gatha's repetition, she experienced the history of her toes, her life. Through her, we did too. Specificity and universality were held in that present moment.

Another student had chosen a gatha, again written by Thich Nhat Hanh, on how to view one's hand to feel the convergence of past and future in the present moment.

> Whose hand is this?
> that has never died?
> Who is it who was born in the past?
> Who is it who will die in the future?[6]

But in the enactment, the student forgot to look at her hand when she recited the words. In her nervousness, she also did not allow herself to breathe. I suggested she begin again, this time gazing at both hands, breathing and giving voice to the text from what she was actually seeing in her own hand. When she repeated the exercise, she used her breath, sight, hand, and the text. She was fully engaged, through her body, in the present moment. This time, the student and the text came alive! This is somatic learning, combining text, action, and full body commitment.

This work with Thich Nhat Hanh's gathas once again reveals the power of using theatre in an academic setting. First, simply being able to memorize a gatha is a new challenge. Second, using one's body to express and communicate opens up new levels of understanding of the text and its concepts. Third, students are encouraged to witness their own shyness or resistance as an act of being in the present moment. Fourth, through concentration and experience, students, for a moment, can enter into Hanh's world of "meaning." Following the enactment of the gathas, the class engages in a discussion of everyday mindfulness and how it connects to Hanh's ideas of interdependence with the past, present, and future.

TECHNOLOGIES OF MEMORY

Memorization is taking the words of an author, or your own words, into your being. Words are not random. In memorizing, we unlock why this phrase is connected to that phrase. We discover thought patterns, why this sentence follows that sentence. We see what is being said, and sense what is not being said.

There are many approaches to how to memorize a text. Here are a few helpful ideas.

- Use a positive intention that you want to remember a text; this frames how you approach the text energetically. "Interest is one of the main factors to be considered in memory; it is the mother of attention, and attention is the mother of memory."[7]
- Visualize—allow the text to offer you an image; that image becomes part of what you are memorizing.
- Speak the words *aloud* many times. Let your eyes scan the words on the page as you hear them internally. "Speak" the words *internally* many times. This constant repetition, in various ways, will allow you to gradually memorize the text.
- Use the text; a text doesn't belong to you until you have used it. When you have memorized the text, write it down many times. Your hand and eye are memorizing the text too. Then use the text in a conversation. Use the text with different physical actions. This solidifies your knowing.
- Kinesiology is also a helpful tool for memorization, concentration and the integration of speech and language. Paul and Gail Dennison have pioneered work in Edu-Kinesthetics, an innovative approach that uses movement as a means to enhance learning. In particular, their "Thinking Cap" exercise and "Energy Yawn" have helped my students in the memorization process.[8]

Memorizing a Gatha

Begin doing the action of the gatha (i.e., brushing your teeth, sweeping). Be aware that you are breathing during the movements. Let the breath and the movement flow together. Keep the action slow in the beginning. Perhaps you will want to experiment with the speed of the actions and how they affect your breathing.

Look at the words of the gatha. Feel out/figure out how the words go with the action. Perhaps you will break down the gatha and its movements into several sections. Keep in mind the meaning of the whole gatha and how the parts of the gatha relate to the whole.

Say the entire gatha out loud with all of the movements/action daily.

When I ask students to enact their gathas in front of the class, I ask each to begin with simply doing the physical action of the gatha and breathing consciously as they do it. I have them repeat the physical action several times so that their bodies are at ease with it. I keep reminding them to breathe as they do this. Concentrating on the breathing and action, the student will gradually lose her or his nervousness and do the work with energy and commitment. Once I see this I ask the student to begin to add the words of the gatha. I may also ask the student to keep repeating the action and the gatha—until I feel the student's relaxed commitment and concentration reflected in her body and voice. In other words, I have the student repeat text and action several times until I feel the student is experiencing "the present moment."

• • •

WRITING AND MEMORIZATION

My first semester at an eastern college found me teaching an introduction to religion course in which half the football team was enrolled. We were halfway through the semester and studying Hinduism. The university's art museum had an exhibition titled "The Goddess in World Religions." A section of the museum held photographs taken in India of the Devi and her immanations: Durga, Kali, Parvati, and Sati. I assigned students to go to the museum, choose a photograph of the Devi, read an article about the representation they had chosen, write a short monologue in her voice, memorize it, and be prepared to enact it. The goal of this exercise, I told students, was to see how each person, male and female, could find and enact the Goddess in herself or himself.

Imagine if you will, a thick muscular hulk standing in front of a photograph of Kali. I ask him to embody the same pose in the photograph. He raises his huge arms to shoulder height with his palms uplifted, and in a deep, gruff voice says: "I am the Goddess Kali. I represent both creation and destruction. I am powerful yet my devotees see me as nurturing and protective. Worship me and I will help you in times of need and traveling." Well, it was quite amazing! Did students laugh? There was a chuckle here and there, but all knew that they could possibly be next. Empathy was the great equalizer.

Another of the football players got up and sat at on the floor at the base of a large photograph of a Kali statue taken in a cave. Just below Kali, on the floor of the cave, was a baby wrapped in white cloths. The football player sat cross-legged, making the motions of holding and rocking a child as he recited his monologue. His voice was soft and he spoke with great care. When he was finished, he looked up and anxiously asked me, "Did you get that I was Kali holding the baby?" Answering for all of us, I assured him that we did "get it" and added how beautiful it was to see the nurturing side of Kali—and yes, his own as well.

Another male student in class wrote :

Worship me
Honor me
Beautiful Warrior
Fight with me for inner peace
Ride with me on my tiger into battle
I will bring you strength and unity of purpose
I am Durga
Worship me
Honor me.

● ● ●

In writing, memorizing, and enacting the Devi I believe male students touched something new in themselves, even for a moment. So did the female students. For the young women of the class to write and speak the words of the Devi I sensed was an affirmation of what they may find difficult to accept in themselves—their power. Whether male or female, each student stood before his or her peers and embodied a Goddess. Each spoke words he or she had written that had become the words of the Devi. Each memorized those words. But simple recitation was not all. It is the combination of memorization and enactment that makes the difference, that deepens the experience, that creates the learning. And what we memorize, what we say often enough and say with our bodies, we can become. At its root, this is a theology of memorization.

Memorization and enactment are further explored in looking at Buddhism through Thich Nhat Hanh's gathas, especially *vipassana* meditation and the experience of the present moment. I use the same method of writing, memorizing, and enacting. As noted above, students memorize and present two gathas, one by Thich Nhat Hanh and also one that they have written and used in their daily lives.

Gathas written and enacted by students

(Said as the student walked across the room)
As I walk to class
I enjoy the air
Which floods all of life.

(Said as the student sat in a chair in front of the class, breathing)
Remember I am your breath
You breathe me
I breathe you
We are one.

(Said as the student stood, looking up, imagining snow falling)
Snowflakes falling on my cheeks
Deep breaths of crisp November air

Cold yet invigorating
I am filled with life.

(Said as the student sat in a classroom chair, imagining looking at a professor)
Looking up, I hear knowledge coming towards me
Closing my eyes sweeps the fog away
Opening my eyes gives knowledge a place.

Student Responses

- For the past week, reciting my gatha daily made me feel more friendly and open. It is peaceful having a "ritual" to recite day after day. Also the gathas are fun and meant for everyday life, making them easier to memorize. It would be interesting to see how many gathas I could memorize and use every day. The gathas bring more meaning to the simple things; making one memorize them brings joy to the day.
- I chose the gatha about "Breathing in I calm my body . . ."[9] It's actually helped me. I get very nervous when I talk in front of a group or in class. I know that I know the material. However, when I go to talk, my mind becomes completely blank. By using this gatha, I breathe, relax, and realize that it is a wonderful moment because I have the opportunity to share my thoughts or work. I know that I am prepared. I've used the gatha before taking a test, or before asking a question in classes. It has helped me tremendously.
- The gathas made me think of my mom. She always taught us to pay attention to our surroundings and to take in the full effect of our actions. I called her and read some of them to her. I really felt the connections of the words with my life.
- The gatha I memorized was about eating mindfully. My life right now is wake up, shower, class/work, eat, class/work, eat, class/work/band. When class and work don't make the day very satisfying, I try to give myself a good meal. So this gatha makes me aware of why I'm eating and [that]I'm grateful to have it.

- I memorized the gatha "Brushing your teeth." When you memorize it and use it in your daily life, it's like a reminder of a sound bit of good advice. It makes you stop for a moment and think about how you should try to be, instead of unthinkingly rushing through your day.
- My gatha was "Breathing in I calm my body . . ." I memorized this before my cross country race on Saturday. So during the race, this came into my mind when I found breathing to be difficult and realized what I already knew: that that moment was wonderful, even though I was in so much pain. After the race, as I lay on the ground gasping, I again realized that I was in a wonderful moment.
- I chose the gatha about driving my car. I find that while I drive I often daydream and get caught up in my thoughts instead of focusing on the moment. Music or a story on NPR can take you away to another place while you drive. It may be safer to focus on driving! But as Thich Nhat Hanh says, focusing on the moment is where happiness is. Not on the future or in the past. So now I drive and focus on being in the moment.

These student reflections attest to the transformative power that enacted, memorized texts, can have. Put another way, these students, for a moment, experienced a practice in *vipassana* Buddhism.

● ● ●

BECOMING THE WORDS

Memorization of religious texts was described earlier in this chapter as an opportunity to enter, for a moment, into the experience of a particular religion. Memorization can also be an avenue to enter into another person's experience. I have worked in the theatre for some twenty years as a theatre director, playwright, and teacher. In the course of teaching acting, I began to notice the power in the act of memorization. Through memorizing a text, one can enter into the spirit of another, be "possessed" by another's words. The paradox in theatre is that the actor is wholly present to herself as well as inhabited by the energies and psyche of her character. This meeting can be so intimate, the union so seamless—I would say it becomes a mystical joining.

Playwright and actress Anna Deavere Smith says: "If you say a word often enough, it becomes you."[10] Smith developed a series of performances that looked at the American psyche through interviews she conducted. She interviewed people involved in the Crown Heights and Los Angeles riots. Two plays resulted from hundreds of interviews, "Fires in the Mirror" and "Twilight: Los Angeles 1992." Each is a solo performance by this African American actress extraordinaire who portrays over thirty different characters, becoming the people that she interviewed, taking on physical identities and accents with split second timing.

> Early on in my work, I wanted to use my body as the evidence that a human being can take on the identity of another. I think we all have immense potential for compassion as individuals. But that gets stopped when we take on fixed positions.[11]

One might say that Anna Deavere Smith, in portraying all of her characters, is expressing the multifaceted parts of her fluid self. Put another way, Smith's portrayals enact the potential in each of us to understand, enter into, and empathize with the other.

Her method is interviewing another with a tape recorder, observing keenly the whole person as she does so (gestures, speech rhythms including ahh's and uh's), transcribing and editing the interview, and memorizing the interview and the physicality of the person.

Rehearsal, practicing over and over, returning to the recorded interview continually, like a touchstone, is her process. What results is Smith's embodied interpretation of another that is also a keen, intuitive observation of that person's core. This mystical joining of self and other is both the challenge and the reward. From this basic process, through the juxtaposition of characters, she tells the multivoiced, multilayered stories of America.

In my teaching, I use Anna Deavere Smith's techniques to guide students into encountering the religious experience of individuals. Words of another hold a piece of that person's identity. By memorizing another's words, a meeting of self and other takes place.

Near the beginning of the semester of my introductory course, I invite three volunteer students to interview religious leaders in the community. I do this early in the course in order to: 1) open up the big questions (e.g., what is religion?), 2) acquaint students with unorthodox methods that will be used throughout the course, 3) place our college course in the context of the larger community, and 4) acquaint students with religious resources in the community. The same students will return to the classroom the following week and "become" those they have interviewed. Using Anna Deavere Smith's methods, the students memorize and perform the responses of the interviewee, becoming them physically through speech, gesture, posture, and actions. I also ask the student to improvise responses (in the style of the interviewee) to questions from the class.

The "performances" are videotaped. Later, I play them for the religious leaders that have given of their time and inspirations. One Presbyterian minister viewed a student who "became" him. He roared with delight, mesmerized by the student's interpretation of him.

In a recent class, a female student "became" a local shaman she had interviewed. The student memorized the words and enacted the physicality of the shaman. The shaman had answered the question, "What is shamanism?" A second student enacted a local Presbyterian minister who had responded to the question, "What is religion?" A third student embodied a local yoga teacher who had answered the question, "What is spirituality?"

This is an excerpt from the Presbyterian minister's interview that was enacted by a male student:

> "I'm just a doubting minister. Doubt can be the fuel for the journey. If you just sit there and accept everything that I'm going to tell you on Sunday, what are you really going to get

> out of it? You're not going to get anything out of it. You have to question, to look; you have to search; you have to find your own answers. That's what it is. I'm not there to give you the answers; that's not my role. My role is to start it up, get you thinking, see how you interact with God, see what you can find. And if you don't want to deal with that right now, that's cool. You might want to put it on the shelf right now. That's fine. I know when I was your age I didn't have all the answers. But the important thing is to search, travel; it's a journey."

Noting the physicality of the interviewee is a key factor in Anna Deavere Smith's method. It is one of the things I encourage students to watch closely during the interview. The gestures, posture, eye focus of a person can reveal a person just as much as that person's spoken words. The student enacting Rev. Mike wore jeans and a T-shirt and sat upright in a chair in front of the class. His legs were wide, his gestures the same, wide and open. His manner was intense, not mincing words, straightforward. He was cool without pushing that he was cool.

The student joined the physicality to what he perceived as an essence of Rev. Mike. He caught a glimpse, inhabited for a moment, of a person who penetrated the viewer with the intensity of someone who hungers for life's search for meaning and demands that of others. The student conveyed him well. Later, the student reflected on becoming the Presbyterian minister: "Interviewing Reverend Mike was an experience that I can carry for the rest of my life, and I am glad that I had the opportunity to conduct this interview with such a great guy."

The student who interviewed the shaman reflected afterward:

> Speaking with Cathy was by far the most rewarding academic experience I have had at college. I have never had to act out the part of another living human being in a classroom setting before, and I think that enhanced everything that I learned from Cathy. When I listened to her speak, I not only listened to her words, but her body language and just the subtle nuances of

> who she was on an introductory level. I thoroughly enjoyed the entire process and I feel that this element of the class should be introduced to other classes as well.

Each student had encountered a spiritual essence of the person they had interviewed. The people they interviewed spoke sincerely, from their hearts. They transmitted feeling. The students received it. Each took the words, physicality, and the indefinable into themselves. Each then represented that person in the classroom. In representing the other, the student had to transmit an essence that lives under and in the words. The student found Rev. Mike to be a no-nonsense pastor who didn't mince words and occasionally even swore to get his point across. The student discovered a place in himself that understood and felt Rev. Mike. Through this empathy, feeling with, he was able to enact an essence of Rev. Mike. The class was astonished and riveted by such a plain-talking minister. They heard, saw, and felt him. They empathized.

Through embodied empathy, the students who represented the shaman, minister, and yoga teacher touched an essential part of the people they interviewed. At the same time, through the process of enacting the other, they met pieces of themselves. Enacting another is a dance of the self and the other. Yes, it is true: "if you say a word often enough it becomes you." But I would add that it is not simply saying something often enough, it is enacting the words with the body's physicality that allows the student to dive into the experience of finding the other within one's self.

THE TECHNIQUE OF THE INTERVIEW

Teacher role

- I call and explain the project to the religious leader/minister. The student is given his/her phone number and is asked to make an appointment.
- I suggest that the student doesn't spend more than a half hour interviewing.

- I create the questions, depending on who is being interviewed. They are large, open-ended questions. Past questions used include: What is religion? What is spirituality? What is God? Students begin with a question and quickly find that it leads to other questions and a real conversation.

Student role

- Take a tape recorder and record the conversation. Try not to interrupt the speaker. If you want to ask another question or make a comment, wait until the speaker finishes his or her thought.
- Listen and observe: listen carefully to the language of the other; observe how a person expresses himself or herself in word and gesture. It's a kind of signature. When thoughts are spoken from the heart, the words and feeling under the words offer the listener an essence of that person. Listen to content and to the spirit contained in the words.
- "Be a sponge" and take in the entire person: words, gestures, postures, actions.

Memorization

- Transcribe the half-hour tape. Keep all the "ah and um's," and pauses. Don't clean it up. You are trying to put on the page the rhythms of how your interviewee speaks. As you put the spoken words down on the page, wherever there is a rhythmic break or change, start a new line. In this way, you will also see the poetic rhythms of your interviewee. During this process of transcription, you will reacquaint yourself with the speaker and recall his/her mannerisms with the spoken word. Remember that words and gestures are tied together. One generates the other.
- Your presentation will be approximately ten minutes. Decide which sections of the interview you will perform. Don't get involved with small edits. Use large chunks of the interview.
- Memorize these sections by hearing the audio tape and seeing the words on the page. Then repeating them yourself trying to maintain the intonation, pauses, intensity, softness, diction, rhythms.

- As you memorize the words, see if you can feel and understand why the speaker says what he/she says. What is the thread that makes each sentence/thought follow each thought? What is not being said?
- Practice without the tape. Using your memory of the physicality of the speaker, take on the body position, standing, sitting or walking; take on the gestures with the words.

Class Enactment

- You have practiced/rehearsed. You are confident of your lines. You may want to bring along with you index cards that outline the flow of thought with key words.
- Following your presentation, the class will ask you—the religious leader—questions. Remain in the character of the interviewee. Use your intuition as to how to answer a question. If you don't know, then just say that. And go on to another question from the class.

CONCLUSION

This chapter has covered a landscape of memorized and enacted sacred texts, spiritual writings by students, and interviews with spiritual leaders. You have been reminded of the age-old technique of memorization that herein is presented as a new pathway to enter religious experience. But the memorization and recitation of texts, writings, and interviews would be of little assistance to pedagogy if it was just that, recitation. Theatre, meaning action and word, activates and deepens the experience of memorization.

The enactment of memorized words propels and allows communication to the rest of the class. This is not mindless recitation. A body moves; words come alive. Word is enfleshed. Observers see, hear, and empathize with another's experience. Perhaps, for a moment, we all experience something larger than ourselves residing in and among us.

6

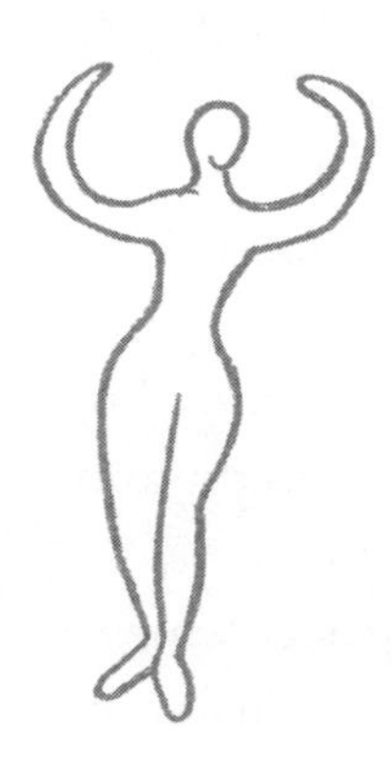

the play is the thing!

Reading and Enacting Dramatic Literature in the Classroom

UP TO THIS POINT we have considered theatre in the classroom as an opening to religious experience. We've seen the use of enactment through theatre techniques as being not merely illustrative of religious ideas, but in fact an embodied moment of contact with religious experience. We now explore the use of dramatic literature in the classroom.

Many others have written of dramatic literature and its ability to make the invisible visible: Peter Brook,[1] Antonine Artaud,[2] Gerardus Van Der Leeuw,[3] to name but a few. Others attest to the incarnational nature of theatre, the word "being made manifest to the senses."[4] Scholars of medieval theatre suggest that art and theatre assisted the growth of one's faith through embodying the stories of Jesus' life.[5] Plays are living books that provide visceral images for the audience more vividly and more unforgettably than any other art form.[6]

In the classroom, I use plays in two ways: to introduce themes of human experience, and to introduce specific religions. You may ask, why not use films? Why plays? Use them all. But use plays to hear the combustion of ideas in the crackle of crystallized language, the sassiness of good dialogue. We don't read plays only for ideas. We read plays for how they are expressed in images, rhythms, and dialogue. In our imagination, we are transported to other worlds. Plays present a world imagined by the playwright and brought to fruition through production and performance.

Plays are written as musical scores are written; they are meant to be seen and heard. The inner dynamics of plays blossom when they are given flesh and blood. They are scores meant to be embodied. At the end of this chapter I will describe how I use plays in the classroom. Here I focus on the reading experience of plays for students.

Reading a play requires imagining the play's environs: the set, costumes, sounds, and action. Here are steps to prepare your students for that experience:

- Read the opening stage directions as if you are an architect imagining how you will design the stage of the theatre for this particular production.

- Characters of the play, when read, are experienced more intellectually than emotionally. Nonetheless, imagine how you think they look. Imagine the tone of voice each character has. See how they gesture and move. Allow them to reveal themselves to you through their dialogue.

- The play, like a score, is a series of impressions, one after the other. They build on one another and need to be experienced that way. Imagine each moment three-dimensionally. If possible read the play in one sitting.

PLAYS OPEN DOORS TO RELIGIOUS THEMES

There is no drama of import that does not have a theological message.

In my introductory course, we read plays to imagine religious themes experienced in everyday life such as faith, pain and suffering, sexuality, and spirituality vs. religion. Playwrights create characters and stories that are shaped by their own spiritualities.

Playwright Migdalia Cruz speaks of this when she says

> The characters in my work are on a journey to find home. Each voyage is like a *hajj*, a search for the place where the divine meets the mundane, a place where a human can speak to a God. Or a Saint. Or a Virgin. I think this is because I think of home existing only when the spiritual world combines with the physical.[7]

Speaking in dialogues and monologues, playwrights wed the mundane to the divine through characters' circumstances. Students enter the world of a character to learn, to be confronted, to discern a new territory, even sometimes to recognize pieces of themselves.

One of the doors I hope to open in religious studies and theology courses is the question, what is faith? It's a prickly place for students who find themselves living their parent's faith, or questioning the need for faith, or perhaps seeking their own. As Kierkagaard suggests, if faith is only possible when we know the pieces of ourselves, then perhaps reading plays is a way to come into conversation with those pieces. Characters' lives and situations open up ways to be in the world. Even if a character's life is one that we would rather not live, it helps in our discernment of how we would like to be in the world.

Students are in the process of developing their own feelings and ideas about faith and meaning. Reading plays can be a way to make the unseen imaginable. Meeting characters who are grappling with similar struggles can give voice to, challenge, and inspire new ways of looking at that important search.

When I select texts to address the question of faith for example, I want the characters to help pry loose students' preconceptions.

Reading plays is a way to startle students' imaginations. Jane Martin's play *Talking With* is a series of monologues by female characters (I find the simplicity of voice and form in monologues particularly helpful for students who are reading plays for the first time). In Martin's play, a baton twirler and a snake handler open the doors into an exploration of the meaning of faith. It is faith at extremes. April's description of watching a baton rise and fall against the sky is the story of her belief system.

> You can't imagine what it feels like to have that baton up in the air. I used to twirl with this girl who called it blue-collar Zen. The "tons" catch the sun when they're up, and when they go up, you go up too. You can't twirl if you're not *inside* the "ton."[8]

April moves from Zen to Christianity as the monologue continues. She describes a wintry day in December, when a select few, "the God-throwers" meet in a certain snowy meadow. Their "clothes fall away" and "acolytes" bring the batons to each thrower.

> They are ebony "tons" with razors set all along the shaft. They are three feet long. One by one the twirlers throw, two "tons" each, thirty feet up, and as they fall back they cut your hands. The razors arch into the air and find God and then fly down to take your blood in a crucifixion, and the red drops draw God on the ground and if you are up with the batons you can look down and see him revealed. Red on white.[9]

The image startles us, makes us cringe. We wonder at April's devotion or is it madness? The reader has been led into her world slowly. The entire monologue presents how she came to baton twirling through her mother. Near the end, she challenges the audience to pick up the baton, to accept the "burden" it represents, to enter "the eye of the needle," which for her is to become the baton and God and human.

Another monologue in *Talking With* presents a snake handler, Caro. She's from a whole family of snake handlers in the Holiness Church. But, different from them, she doesn't believe in God after seeing her mother die from a snake bite. Instead, her faith comes from another place inside her. At her mother's funeral, she was snake handling when she realized it. The snake . . .

> started to leverage. So I said, "Snake. You Satan's handmaiden. You're right, there ain't no God in me. I'm just a woman, but I'm the only woman in my Dada's house and he needs me home. Outta his faith and his need, you lock yer jaws." I let that snake feel a child's pure love and it sponged it up offa my hands and then ol'wiggley went limp. I tranced it. . . . Yes, you got to believe. Holiness Church is dead right about that. Makes me wonder, you know? I git to lookin' at people and wonderin' if they got anything in 'em could lock a serpent's jaws. Any power or spirit or love or whatever. . . . Maybe you can handle and maybe you can't, but there's but one sure thing in this world . . . yer empty, yer gonna git bit.[10]

I am always amazed at that last line, "yer empty, yer gonna git bit." She could be talking about faith in the Divine, self-belief, courage, passion. For anyone, Caro's words take us deep inside to hear our own answers to her challenge.

These two monologues from *Talking With* are occasions for self-reflection as well as class discussion. Often, after reading them aloud in class, I ask students to "free write" a stream of conscious response. For class discussion I offer these questions:

- These two characters—the baton twirler and snake handler—are extreme examples. What do you learn about a faith experience from them?
- Are the characters' actions tests of their faith in the Divine or tests of their faith in themselves?
- Is faith a series of "survivor" tests?
- What does ordinary, everyday life have to do with faith?

To open the discussion of what is a search for meaning in life, I offer a camping experience in two different plays. Several years ago, a dear friend, Letitia Bartlett, a clown and mime, and I collaborated on writing a play about the search for mysticism in everyday life. We called it *Ecstasy in the Everyday*. In the main character's search for meaning in her life, we see a woman encounter obstacles in daily meditation, in the weekly clean-up of her apartment, in her relationship with her bird, at work with her boss, and in a camping trip.

> I'm so distracted. I can't concentrate. I gotta get out of the city. The grabbing, the over-achieving over achievers! I get in the car, head north. San Rafael, Novato, Petaluma. I see the cows, the trees, it's green, it's beautiful.
>
> *Music: Hildegard of Bingen*
>
> I'm in a cathedral of redwoods! I say to myself, I just want a little peace, a little open space. I want to find something, a blessing, a moment of grace . . . I want a blessing. (Music goes out.) So I find this perfect spot in the redwoods to sit, as if an architect from Architectural Digest had designed this perfect spot for me (she sits). And here's a perfect arm rest, and a perfect foot stool. And I lean back (she sighs). Ugh, I need something for my back (she looks). If I scoot over here I can lean back . . . oooh, that feels good. But I need something for my neck. I know, I'll make a pillow of redwood needles (she does). Oh, yes, it feels good. I think I could come here on a regular basis. This could be my spot. I could bring some food, water, a little table. I could set up an easel and do some painting! I could spend the night here, bring my sleeping bag, my mat, reading materials, a lamp, a cooler . . . I could cook dinner out here! Food tastes so good when you cook outside! I could invite those nice people I met at that workshop and we could all get to know each other better! . . . And all of a sudden, I say, "What am I thinking?" I come here to the forest for a blessing, and I'm building a

> house! I'm building a whole housing development! No wonder I can't find any space, I keep filling it up with wants! Wanting, well, it's good for the economy, right?
>
> *Music: Hildegard of Bingen*
>
> All of a sudden I feel this breeze come into me (pause, as slides of interiors of cathedrals are projected on her body). I feel so full, so present, like my boundaries have relaxed, and a part of me is the forest, and a part of the forest is me. And I realize, I have the blessing, I've always had the blessing. It's me . . . it's in me.[11]

The woman's wants mirror our consumer society focused on external values, often overwhelming our inner sense of who we are or the meaning of life. The music of Hildegard von Bingen is a speechless moment in which the sacred within the woman and outside her seeks to be heard. When we read the speech out loud in class, I play a contemporary interpretation of Hildegard's music by Richard Souther, "Vision."

In a one-act play, *The Singing of the Stars* by Libyan playwright Ahmed Ibrahim Al-Fagih, a couple camps overnight in the wilderness. They are preparing to leave in the morning, putting away the bedding, food items. They share a piece of cake together.

WOMAN: There's no pollution in the air here to spoil food the way it spoils everything else in life. Look how you feel when you wake up here—full of energy, so cheerful and fresh, life seeming so wonderful. How lucky we were to stumble on this place. . . . I had some beautiful dreams. If I tell you something, will you promise not to laugh?

MAN: Say it and don't ever stop. But don't stop me laughing. When I'm with you, I want to laugh. I want to play around, feel free to throw off all the sadness and pain and depression my heart was full of before I met you.

WOMAN: Would you believe me if I told you how, last night, I thought I heard the singing of the stars? And that their singing was so beautiful?

MAN: Of course I'd believe you. We couldn't all have gone on living our lives, here on earth, if we hadn't been guided by the stars. They watch over us from the cradle to the grave . . .

WOMAN: The tune was so full of happiness. The stars were singing to me about love, asking me to be their guest. They were offering me food from their celestial tables, holding out a cup of heavenly light. I'll try and remember the tune. It goes like this.

(She laughs as she hums the tune, dancing and clapping her hands. The man dances and claps along with her, repeating the tune. They laugh and fling themselves into one another's arms).[12]

Amidst a wondrous time, the dialogue reveals that they are having an affair; the woman is married. Soon the man and woman are interrupted by a voice shouting "Danger. Danger. Don't move." The voice warns them that they are standing in the middle of a minefield, abandoned after the war. One step further might be the end of both of them. The voice says he will go and tell the authorities to rescue them. The couple surmises that since they arrived after dark, they hadn't seen the posted warning signs. As the love feast disintegrates into terror, they blame one another for coming to this spot. The authorities return (voices heard offstage), and with them arrive the television reporters (all voices from offstage). They ask if the couple heard the ghosts of the dead the previous night. The man responds that all they heard was "the singing of the stars."

VOICE OF THE NEWS CORRESPONDENT: Did you say the singing of the stars?

MAN: Yes, the ones up there in the sky. The ones you can't see at the moment, because they're as clever at disguising themselves and vanishing as they are at playing music and singing. They sang beautifully last night.

VOICE OF THE NEWS CORRESPONDENT: The viewers would be fascinated to know what this singing was like. Do you remember the tune the stars sang for you?[13]

The man begins singing the tune he heard earlier. The woman joins him. They begin to move and dance and sing as they had in the beginning. The authorities and camera people scream not to move because they will blow everyone up—including themselves. The man and woman continue ecstatically singing, the screams of the people offstage rise higher. The screaming and the singing continue, as the curtain falls.

Both plays, *Ecstasy in the Everyday* and *The Singing of the Stars,* suggest what can happen in a search for meaning when we listen to the life around us and within us. For the woman in *Ecstasy*, the act of listening awakens her inner life. While the ending of *The Singing* leaves it open for our interpretation, the man and woman seem to return to belief/meaning in the song of the stars, the cosmos, the divine, their love. As they sing, the melody seems to protect them from the buried mines, keeps them dancing over the minefields of life despite the opposition of the world.

Questions for class discussion

- In each of these plays, how do the characters search for meaning?
- What is the significance of music in each play?
- How does the act of listening influence all of the characters?
- What does listening have to do with a search for meaning?
- Where have you searched for meaning in your life? (a free write)

If home, as playwright Migdalia Cruz has said, is encountered when the spiritual and physical worlds touch, then when flesh and blood meet the Divine, closets are opened in patriarchal religious traditions. The subjects of gender, sex, and sexuality have been avoided, perceived as abhorrent, or simply silenced by many patriarchal religions. In the 1980s, the advent of the pandemic of AIDS forced many religions to openly address sex and sexuality. In this day, pedophilia, homophobia, and misogyny in the Roman Catholic Church and elsewhere warn us that though the road is long it is utterly urgent to reimagine sex-positive and body-positive theologies.

The Pulitzer Prize winning play by Tony Kushner, *Angels in America: A Gay Fantasia on National Themes,* opens many doors thematically. Part One is entitled "Millennium Approaches," Part Two, "Perestroika." Kushner offers a searing tale of primarily men, some caught in fear of their homosexuality, others celebrating it, and still others frightened by the meaning of love in relation. Louis, who is Jewish, has deserted his partner with AIDS. Louis speaks his fear to the closeted Joe, who is a Mormon.

> Maybe we are free. To do whatever. Children of the new morning, criminal minds. Selfish and greedy and loveless and blind. Reagan's children. You're scared. So am I. Everybody is in the land of the free. God help us all.[14]

How crucial it is for students to hear (and, yes, you can also rent the video of it) and see the complexity and beauty of sexualities, the rainbow. Because *Angels in America* is a brilliant play, it has many levels of themes that your students will encounter such as forgiveness, prejudice and stigma, truth, lying and coming out of the closet, politics and community. The play gives emphasis to two religions, Judaism and Mormonism. Class discussion can begin with how each of these traditions articulates (or not) a position on same-sex relationships. For an overview of the play, there is a good website: www.sparknotes.com/drama/angels.

The fear of women's sexuality is often at the root of religious fears to embrace a sex-positive and body-positive theology. Caryl Churchill's play *Vinegar Tom,* set in seventeenth-century Britain, looks at the burning of witches. Each woman in the play is accused of witchcraft because of her intelligence, her individuality, and, worst of all, her sexuality. Women are persecuted in the world of *Vinegar Tom* because men are afraid of them and they are afraid of themselves. Women in the play are told that they are evil. Some of them scream out in valiant opposition, while others, eager to please or desperate to be cured of this evil, start to believe it. The play collapses the Christian church's sordid history with the *Malleus Maleficarum* or

Hammer of Witches with the demonization of contemporary women's sexuality in its final lyrics:

Evil Women
Is that what you want?
Is that what you want to see?
On the movie screen
Of your wet dream
Evil Women

Evil Women
Is that what you want?
Is that what you want to see?
In your movie dream
Do they scream and scream?
Evil Women
Evil Women[15]

The reclamation of lesbian sexuality and spirituality is seen in *Landscape of My Body,* a play I wrote in 1988 at Union Theological Seminary. The play reclaims women's bodies as sacred and questions a disembodied mysticism. Here two women playfully discover each other:

INGRID: What do you see?

MARGARET: I see you.
A cathedral (her hand sculpts the air around her body)
Round rosetta windows (her hand sculpts the air around her breasts)
A round dome (her hand sculpts the air around her head)
Graceful arches (rib cage and arms)
A tabernacle (torso)

INGRID : You see a church?

MARGARET: A church, wholly a church (she genuflects).
What do you see?

INGRID: I see light and shadow
Circles within circles
Spirals of votive candles
Nooks and naves of cathedrals

MARGARET: You see inside me like a church?

INGRID: Beautiful woman . . .

MARGARET: Beautiful woman . . .[16]

The play opens the door to reclaim women's beauty, and by extension, opens the names of the sacred to include female images. If women's bodies are "church," then their love relationships—homosexual, bisexual, heterosexual, and transgendered—can be the occasion to embody the Divine in the world.

Looking at human relationship is a means of looking at our relationship with the Divine. To open this door, we use my play, *CancerBodies*. The play explores how suffering and celebration can be held in tension within relationship. Partially adapted from *Cancer in Two Voices,* the character of Barbara is diagnosed with breast cancer. Her partner Sandy struggles to support her.[17] A curandera/healer poetically offers alternative views to Western medicine. A multifaith cancer support group enlarges the pandemic of the disease to different ages, religions, and ethnicities. In this scene, in the face of Barbara's worsening condition, Barbara and Sandy create their own commitment ritual using elements of the traditional Jewish wedding ceremony.

DR. GRANT: I don't have good news. The cancer has metastasized to your liver.

SANDY: We need to exhort the heavens. "L'Chaim. To life!" We need to begin again.

JANE: We raise the chupah and ask Sandy and Barbara to stand beneath it . . . to create a place together that symbolizes home, the sides open in welcome to all those who would enter and join them there.

BARBARA (speaking to the audience): Sandy has wanted this commitment ceremony for years. I've always been ambivalent about rituals. But now, I feel ready to create a ritual that honors us.

JANE (motions to the other women to surround Sandy and Barbara): During the ring ceremony we will ring you in community.

BARBARA: Sandy, our relationship is one of the major accomplishments of my life. I came to understand so many things. I came to understand that the struggle to negotiate differences is itself a type of commitment. You have expanded my notions of a moral, ethical, and political life. You have made me feel beautiful and special, and I grew to become special to myself and to other people. I have learned what it's like to be loved unconditionally. This ring represents the unbroken circle of life and the completeness of our bond.

SANDY: Barbara, you have taught me much of what I have come to value about myself. You have taught me how to play and to sing 1930s medleys in the night. You have watched relievedly as I grew brave enough to look away from your wounds and toward my own. You have opened and softened my heart. In your love, I have found a home. In your love, I have created community and family. In your love, I have learned to love myself. This ring symbolizes the delicacy and strength of Barbara as well as the delicacy and strength of our love.

(Klezmer music. Barbara and Sandy hold ends of a handkerchief and dance.)

DOCTOR (stepping between them and interrupting the dance): Catheter put in groin. Check to see if portals are open . . .[18]

Rather than the pain of isolation and rejection that so many experience with cancer, the theology of the play suggests that changes in the body, whether from age or disease, embraced with love and compassion, keep a person connected to a larger sense of self, to the world, and to the sacred.

Angels in America, Vinegar Tom, Landscape of My Body, and *CancerBodies* are plays that open the door to themes of gender, sexuality, and spirituality: gay and lesbian sexuality in light of religious traditions and women's sexuality and our relationship to ourselves, others, and the Divine. These plays offer students the multifaceted faces of women and men living out loud. Students understand that the body, sex, and sexuality are everyday experiences not separate from religious life, but that, in fact, fuel it.

Students are assigned to read each of these play texts. We also read portions of them in class. Each play offers avenues for discussion. Here are a few of the questions I have used to begin reflections:

- Why is it important to address the body as a religious issue?
- Can you imagine your body as church, as mosque, synagogue, temple?
- What does one's gender have to do with religion?
- What was your mother's or grandmother's experience of religion?
- What do religious traditions have to say about sexuality?
- What would the Angel of *Angels in America* say to the women of *Vinegar Tom*?
- How are we to bear physical or mental suffering? What do religions tell us about how to endure suffering?
- Sandy and Barbara, in the face of Barbara's death, create a commitment ceremony using a symbol, the chupah, of their shared Judaism. What does celebration bring to the experience of suffering?

PLAYS THAT OPEN DOORS TO RELIGIONS

Above, we looked at using plays to encounter religious themes. Here I want to offer you brief descriptions of plays that I use to help students encounter a particular religion. It is important to state that each of the plays I've selected is used to deepen the introduction of a religion to students. They are read either in whole or in part and are accompanied by scholarly readings that contextualize and articulate the beliefs and practices of each religion.

In courses, I use the poetic and passionate plays of Al-Sabur, Thich Nhat Hanh, Eric Ehn, Kahlil Gibran, S. Ansky, and Merle Feld, along with myriads of storytellers who created the Mahabharata. These playwrights call out the imaginations of students, leading them through the doorways of mosques, churches, temples, and monasteries into the lived practices and beliefs of the world's religions.

Judaism

The Dybbuk by S. Ansky, also known as *Between Two Worlds,* is the most often performed play of world Jewish theatre. It opens doors into Jewish mysticism and the Kabbalah, earthly existence and the sacred. The covenant of the Torah between the Holy and the Jewish people, between the Holy and humanity, is intact. All of the characters, particularly the *dybbuk*, are instruments of a loving and just Divinity who continues to watch over and care for creation. It's a comforting thought for any age and, perhaps, it helps explain the continued popularity of Ansky's extraordinary play.

Between Two Worlds (The Dybbuk) involves ill-fated Jewish lovers in Eastern Europe. Khonnon, a poor devout student of Jewish mysticism, adores Leah, and they plan to marry. However, her father breaks off their engagement to wed her to a wealthier man. When Khonnon learns of this, he dies immediately. His soul is transformed into a dybbuk that inhabits Leah's body to keep her for himself. A rabbi is finally able to exorcise the dybbuk using ritual, incantation, and blasts of the shofar. Leah must ultimately choose between a loveless marriage and an unworldly union with Khonnon's spirit.

Merle Feld's cogent and passionate play *Across the Jordan* juxtaposes the Genesis story of Sarah and Hagar (the mothers of the Jewish and Arab races) with the contemporary situation of Israelis and Palestinians. The play movingly attests that the daughters and sons of Sarah and Hagar are all the children of Abraham. The biblical story between these two women (including the midrash) is played out simultaneously with a modern day Hagar and Sarah. The reader meets Najah, in prison and under suspicion for throwing a bomb. Hers is a palpable longing "to feel my mother's hand on my face . . . to sit in my olive grove and be with those old trees."[19] She is both the modern-day Hagar and Ishmael. The contemporary Sarah/Isaac is Daphna, who is studying the Torah for her deceased father and is also an attorney representing Najah. Daphna finds her own independence and power, unlike the biblical Sarah, who in the end is alone and destroyed. *Across the Jordan* opens doors of understanding to the importance of origins, family, and tradition within Judaism. It also embodies the divisions between Israelis and Palestinians seen through the eyes of women while simultaneously offering visions of peace between the daughters of Abraham.

Christianity

Monologues allow students easy access to stories and characters. Kahlil Gibran's *Jesus the Son of Man* is a provocative introduction for students to the life of Jesus. Gibran uses the literary gesture of writing a series of first-person accounts (monologues) as if by persons who knew Jesus. The characters, such as Mary Magdalen, Pilate's wife, and Joseph of Arimathaea, give the reader a fresh picture of Jesus, and the relationships he had. Rachel, a disciple of Jesus remembers him this way: "He loved us with a tender love. His heart was a winepress. You and I could approach with a cup and drink there from."[20] Because so many have written of Jesus, students find Gibran's approach refreshing, poetic, and accessible.

At once provocative and lyrical, Eric Ehn's *The Saint Plays* allow students to meet the pantheon of Catholic saints in contemporary life.[21] As Celia Wren writes of Ehn's series of short plays, they are

> remarkable pieces of "exploded biography" (as their author puts it) that range widely in length, historical specificity and crypticness. "A saint is a human mandala–a life in a ritual

> shape held up as a focus for contemplation," Ehn wrote in his provocative and slightly opaque preface to the anthology The Saint Plays. . . . In *The Freak*, a girl born with wings baptizes the shoe of a knight she meets in a dream—the story commemorates the dragon-killing St. George. *Thistle*, dedicated to St. Rose of Lima, revolves around a witness's description of a 1990 massacre in El Mozote, El Salvador. And in *Pain*, the tragedy of a missing child in contemporary New York parallels the story of the third-century Spanish martyr St. Eulalia.[22]

Ehn's plays startle us with dreams and heroic lives lived amidst tyranny and everyday struggles. In class, we use these short plays to discuss the notion of sainthood and whether saints model something that is useful for students today.

Hinduism

In chapter 5 I described students who memorized and gave voice to the dialogue between Arjuna and Krishna in the second and twelfth books of the Bhagavad Gita. For me, reading the entire dialogue of the Gita is the most profound experience of Hindu dramatic literature. Recalling ideas from the Upanishads, the Gita balances mysticism and the practical needs of daily life. Action and duty are integral to the spiritual path. As the Gita says, "the wise see knowledge and action as one."[23] Since whole courses are based on the Bhagavad Gita, in my work I rarely have students encounter the entire text. Instead, students read portions of it and portions of the larger work that frames the *Gita*, the *Mahabharata*. The play *The Mahabharata* by Jean-Claude Carriere and Peter Brook focuses on the theme of apocalypse. Carriere describes the play thus: "the theme is a threat: we live in a time of destruction—everything points in the same direction. Can this destruction be avoided?"[24] Though his perspective does not focus on the transformative nature of this sacred text, for Western students living in these times of "endless wars" this interpretation by Carriere and Brook calls to us with foreboding.

Buddhism

The Buddhist call to peacemaking is richly represented in the work of Vietnamese Buddhist monk Thich Nhat Hanh. "To preserve peace our hearts must be at peace with our brothers and sisters. When we try to overcome evil with evil, we are not working for peace."[25] During the Vietnam War, four young Vietnamese men were shot and killed in the village of Binh Phuoc. They were volunteer workers in the School of Youth for Social Service, "a nonviolent organization that sought only to heal the wounds of war and reconstruct villages."[26] In Hanh's one act play *The Path of Return Continues the Journey,* the four youth are paddled upstream in a boat by Mai, who months earlier immolated herself for the cause of peace.[27] During the journey, the youth tell the story of their deaths and find compassion for their murderers. The play frames Buddhist responses to questions such as: Where do we come from and where do we go? What separates the living from the dead? What is living? What is death? What is peace? It is an eloquent, poetic play that introduces students to Hanh's work and to the deep need our world has for being peace. Daniel Berrigan writes in the introduction:

> The ironies implicit in the play are enormous and far of reach. We Americans cross the great waters with our techniques of death. . . . And lo, coming across those same waters . . . comes another sort of craft, peopled with spirits, listening, bantering, remembering, laughing. Their wounds are healed, their memories lucid.[28]

Islam

Sufism is juxtaposed to Islamic orthodoxy in Salah 'Abd al-Sabur's two-act play *Murder in Baghdad.* It is based on the life of Persian mystic al-Hallaj, who lived during the ninth and tenth century, C.E. Al-Hallaj taught and lived in Baghdad. As a Sufi mystic he taught the union of the Beloved and himself, "And he, the Almighty, is in every man without distinction; He is Light . . ." [29] Al-Hallaj's immanent God is in opposition to the orthodox transcendent God. Revered as a Sufi martyr, al-Hallaj was crucified on a tree branch not because he preached against the poverty caused by injustice but because he divulged the sacred mystery of his oneness with God. The play offers students a passionate picture of Sufi mysticism. Further, the question arises, is it al-Hallaj's longing for his Beloved that inevitably results in his martydom, or is his death rather a punishment for the sin he has committed by divulging his relationship with the Beloved? *Murder in Baghdad* is a story that offers students a moving vision of the experience of direct union with God that is present in all mysticisms. Al-Hallaj expresses the beauty of this relationship for Islam.

HOW I USE PLAYS IN THE CLASSROOM

I use the plays introduced above in various ways. Sometimes, I will only assign certain scenes from a play to be read. Whether students have read a play in whole or in part, prior to beginning our class discussion, I ask for volunteers to read aloud scenes or monologues from it. This not only refreshes the play in their minds, but also allows students to experience the language, noting the difference between reading it themselves and hearing it aloud. If I want us to experience more of the play, I split the class into small groups. Each group "rehearses" a scene from the play and then we read them aloud in succession. In that situation, it is often very informative and revealing to have several students playing the same role.

I have often found that women students in particular are empowered by reading plays aloud. Initially hesitant, with encouragement and with continued repetition of the reading aloud, women students find more confidence in their own voices through reading another's voice. Sometimes this also means reading across gender. For example, in *Angels in America,* I often assign women to read the role of Roy Cohen (a fast-talking, manipulative attorney), or in *Murder in Baghdad* the role of al-Hallaj. I find that male students are often too threatened to read the gay roles in *Angels in America.* Women students reading the Louis/Pryor or Louis/Joe scenes open up the possibility of "hearing" the play. Having men read the women's roles in *Talking With* allows female students to experience the roles differently as well.

Reading plays aloud is an experience of language that is vibrant, that communicates. For both male and female students, the dialogue of plays can offer new models for how people express themselves.

Other ideas for using plays

- As part of chapter four, I described the technique of interviewing characters. It can be used here to interview the characters of a play in order to further explore an issue or idea. Assign several students the same character to study in their reading of a play. Interview all of them, singly or all at once, in order to experience the various points of view that one character might hold.
- Also in chapter four, I discussed the use of improvisation. To further explore a situation and its characters once the class has read a play, students can improvise a scene in their own words. You may want to also ask a group of students to study a scene and present alternative solutions to the characters' dilemma.

THEATRES AS RESOURCES

A couple of years ago, I became aware of a unique project being developed at the Cornerstone Theatre Company in Los Angeles.[30] Cornerstone's Faith-Based Theater Cycle is a five-year series exploring how faith can unite people—and divide them. In a series of residencies, the company collaborated with communities of faith throughout Los Angeles. Some of the projects engage people who share a religion, others are interfaith projects, some include a single congregation, and still others invite those who are not active participants in organized religion to reflect on the meaning of faith. From these collaborations six plays have emerged as of this writing. Each of these plays would be evocative assignments for students as entry points into the faiths depicted.

Center of the Star: A Jewish Walking Tour of Los Angeles
You Can't Take It with You: An American Muslim Remix
Order My Steps (an African American gospel musical)

Crossings (Catholic immigrants in five parishes)
Body of Faith (homosexuality, faith, identity)
As Vishnu Dreams (Hinduism, a contemporary Ramayana)

One of the outstanding Jewish theatre companies in the United States is the Traveling Jewish Theatre. It is a source of further plays that embody and articulate the Jewish faith and experience.[31]

• • •

It is my hope that this chapter offers a small footpath to the vast storehouse of dramatic plays that awaits religious studies professors, theologians, and all those involved in religious education. In the spirit of blessings, I offer the following to each of you:

May curious, imaginative teachers seek new dramatic directions as pedagogical paths.

May you take the plays off their shelves, read them, delight in them and give them flesh in your classrooms.

May you feel creative winds at your back, urging you forward to explore through dialogue and story the struggles and joys of faith in our everyday lives.

Whether read aloud in a classroom setting, spirituality group, or read silently, may you experience the lively discussions that will flow from the pages of dramas.

May students, through empathy with characters and their situations, find themselves enthusiastically engaged in the thrill of new methods of learning.

May you and your students use dramatic literature in your classrooms to challenge and embolden the all too predictable terrain that threatens to anesthetize the crucial study of religions.

7

evaluating students through enactment and playwriting

THROUGHOUT THIS BOOK I present theatre techniques that enflesh the teaching of religion. These methods inherently blur the false dichotomy of body and mind. Theatre is action inspired by our imaginations. In this book you see students become a character, express an idea by becoming a sculpture, enact sacred texts, and feel the interconnections of body-mind-spirit in moving to music. And so the classroom becomes an arena for experience, for witnessing the experience of others, and for reflection.

But how do you evaluate experience? In this pedagogy, experience is both an inner and outer journey. And each journey feeds and flows into the other. With my teaching, it is my hope that students touch new parts of their interior life through reflection. They bring their inner experience (e.g., memorized sacred texts) into external experience through classroom enactments. When students study Buddhism, for example, and the work of Thich Nhat Hanh, they memorize a gatha (see chapter 5) and use it in their daily lives. Also in chapter 5, you read student comments about the process of memorizing and enacting the gathas. In their reflections, you saw the flow between the inner experience of the gatha and their everyday lived experience of it.

But how to evaluate these inner and outer journeys? It is only appropriate that in using theatre as pedagogy in religious studies and theology, the methods of the theatre, enactment and playwrighting, should become primary evaluative tools.

For the most part, assessing the student's inner experience is done through reflection papers in my courses. In assessing the outer, the process of enactment itself becomes the tool for evaluation. What is enactment? It is fully experienced knowledge. It is the integration of body-mind-spirit. I use the word enactment in stark contrast to theatre performance, which must communicate a play and must rely on character portrayal, a complex system of rehearsal, character research, and skills such as diction and movement. Enactment shares with performance full body expression and communication of ideas. But its goal is not performance, nor is it therapy. Enactment is focused on the individual student deepening, enlarging, and amplifying the integration of scholarship and embodiment. It is wholistic in its combination of thought and action, body and mind. Wholistic learning is enacted knowledge. Thus assessment must be focused on individual progress in progressive enactments for each student.

Learning Outcomes

The ability to assess students' work begins on the first day of a class with clearly articulated intentions and enactments. The learning outcomes in my syllabus to Introduction to World Religions map areas of competence that will result from the cross pollination of theatre, religious studies/theology, and religious experience.

- Students will be conversant with the major ideas of Hinduism, Buddhism, Judaism, Christianity, and Islam.
- Through theatre, students will viscerally acquire knowledge of religious experience.
- Through theatre, students will experience wholistic learning through enacted knowledge. Enactment is fully experienced knowledge.

Assignments

The assignments are presented to offer students an overview of the kind of work they will generate in the course.

- Class readings
- Participation in classroom theatre exercises, improvisations
- Interviewing, editing, memorization of the interview, enactment
- Memorization and enactment of sacred texts
- Creative writing—poetry and dialogues
- Presentations by each student—there will be two student presentations at each class meeting
- Final paper: research, scene writing, and analysis

It is one thing to read the learning outcomes and typical assignments in the syllabus. It is quite another to "walk our talk" and get on our feet and experience theatre/body exercises the first day (described in chapter 2). But "tasting" the course the first day is crucial for students. Building on a clear presentation of goals and methods, the basis for evaluation is clarified.

In my introductory course, I don't individually assess students' participation in group warm-ups and theatre exercises (such as those described in chapter 2). Instead, I consider the exercises opportunities for students to learn new ways of expressing themselves. These theatre exercises are barometers for me as a teacher to gauge class energy, involvement, and mood.

EVALUATING IMPROVISATION

There are several theatre techniques in this book that, for assessment's sake, I will place under the umbrella of improvisation, including sculpting (chapter 3), movement exercises to enflesh character, group interviews of a character, improvisations with a partner (chapter 4). The overall motif for evaluation of these improvisations is: Does the student enter into the exercise with energy and commitment? Sharing ahead of time with students the areas for assessment helps to focus their work:

- Energy and full body commitment (to the extent that the student is able) to the exercise
- Is the student speaking clearly for all to hear? The audience/class is an integral part of the work.
- Is the student working with his partner(s): listening and responding, allowing for a give and take, an exchange, of dialogue?
- Is the student relating to her partner with her eyes and body language?
- If applicable, is the student able to integrate into the content of the improvisation ideas from class readings in addition to his own ideas?

EVALUATING ENACTMENT OF TEXTS

In what follows, I am offering evaluative methods for interviewing, writing and enacting monologues, memorization of sacred texts, and the final paper. While I use traditional assessment methods such as pop quizzes, and a mid-term to help accomplish the learning outcomes, enactment itself is the primary evaluative method of the course. I offer students weekly opportunities to enact knowledge, which places this method at the center of the course. It also gives students multiple vantage points from which to view the method. During the first class meeting, I ask students to sign up for presentations throughout the semester, two per class session. Some of the sign up slots are weighted toward traditional research and oral presentation, but most use theatre enactment as a way to gauge a student's learning.

Presentation Sign-up List

1. Three Student Presentations:
   Each student will conduct a 30-minute interview based on a provided theme/question. The student will take notes, and possibly audio record the interview. The student will prepare an 8–10 minute monologue in which s/he memorizes the words of the interview and embodies the person interviewed. This will be followed by a 10-minute question and answer period in which the student will respond to questions (in character) from the class. A reflection paper on this process will be due the following week.

   - Interview Rev. Mike, Presbyterian Church: "What is religion?" Embody him in front of the class. Reflection paper on the process—1 page
   - Interview Cathy, shaman: "What is shamanism?" Embody her in front of the class. Reflection paper on the process—1 page
   - Interview Charlie, spiritual teacher and yoga instructor: "What is spirituality?" Embody him in front of the class. Reflection paper on the process—1 page

2. Two Student Presentations: (10–15 minutes each)

   - History of Yom Kippur: What is it? How did it originate? What are the religious practices?—1 page due after the presentation
   - History of Rosh Hashanah: What is it? How did it originate?, What are the religious practices?—1 page due after the presentation

3. Two Student Presentations:
    - Write a contemporary monologue for the character of "Sarah" (1 page). Memorize the monologue and embody the character for the class.
    - Write a contemporary monologue for the character of "Hagar" (1 page). Memorize the monologue and embody the character for the class.
4. Assignment: ALL: do two (2) interviews of other students: Ask "What is Christianity?"
    - Write their words down afterwards, memorize them, and in class be prepared to embody them.
5. Assignment ALL:
    - Memorize a portion of a sura of the Qur'an and be prepared to embody it.
    - Interview two students: "What do you know about Islam?"
    - Memorize their responses and embody/ "become" them.
6. Two Student Presentations:
    - Rumi: Memorize a poem, present it, and reflect on it.—1 page
7. Two Student Presentations: 10–15 minute each
    - Menon/Shweder: "Power in its Place: Is the Great Goddess of Hinduism a Feminist?" - Oral presentation of the article, and 1 page reflection paper
    - Pintchman: "Is the Hindu Goddess Tradition a Good Resource for Western Feminism?"—Oral presentation of the article, and 1 page reflection paper
8. Two Student Presentations:
    - Upanishads: Memorize a section, embody it, and reflect on it.—1 page

9. Assignment ALL :
   - Memorize a "gatha," of Thich Nhat Hanh.
   - Use it in your daily life.
   - Write a gatha of your own and memorize it.
   - Be prepared to embody Hanh's and your own gatha in class.
10. Two Student Presentations:
    - Research: Who is Thich Nhat Hanh? A biography—1 page
    - Research: Buddhism in the United States: Why is it so popular?—1 page
11. Assignment ALL:
    - Read: *Being Peace,* p. 63, reread the "I Am . . ." poem and write one of your own using the format that Hanh uses; memorize your own, and be very familiar with Hanh's poem as well. Be prepared to enact them in class.

INTERVIEWS

In the sign-up for #1 in the preceding sign-up sheet, three students volunteer to present their interviews with local religious leaders during a class session. As described in chapter 5, the presentation involves interviewing, editing, memorization, performance, and reflection.

Besides being a precise method of communicating, theatre is also an evaluative tool. Evaluation of the assignment is based upon what is communicated. Having done the interview, edited, and memorized it, the student expresses the thoughts, feelings, and physicality of another. The success of the student's work is based upon how well it is communicated.

EVALUATING INTERVIEWS

- Has the student memorized the text of the interview (rather than improvised a quasi-rendition/facsimile of the interviewee)?

  Note: ask the student to give you a copy of the edited interview before the enactment; ask another student to follow the text of the written interview during the enactment in order to offer forgotten lines and/or be asked afterward how well the presenting student did in terms of sticking to the text. It's also advisable for you to receive a copy of the interview afterwards.

- Does the student communicate the person interviewed—in voice, language, gesture, body?
- The audience/class is an integral part of this work. Is the student speaking clearly for all to hear? (If the student is rushing her words, ask her to speak more slowly, and breathe!)
- In the question and answer period following the presentation of the interview, students can ask the "interviewee/character" anything. If something is asked beyond the presenting student's experience or knowledge of the character they are portraying, I suggest they say "I don't know." Otherwise, the questions and answers are an improvisatory moment that reveal how the student integrates and reflects the interviewee.
- In the oral and written reflection, does the student articulate an understanding of the topic (e.g., what is religion?) 1) because of the interview and 2) through the experience of enacting the interviewee?

In evaluating the work, a word of caution: stay focused on your evaluation points. There will be many "side issues" thrown up to distract you. Enactment does that: nervousness, moments of memory failure, perhaps hearing the student is difficult (in which case, ask the student to speak up). These distractions from the enactment can be noted, but should not negatively affect the evaluation.

In this assignment and others like it, I am not looking for a searing portrayal by a great actor. I am looking to see if this student, shy or boisterous, communicates what she has experienced. Whatever she does, it will be an interpretation of the person interviewed. Does the student make contact with herself and present an interpretation of the "other" through her own person? In the situation offered in chapter 5, is some rough essence of Rev. Mike felt by you the witness? If so, the student is succeeding. Is the student able, in the improvisatory question and answer period, to integrate Rev. Mike's persona and his general ideas? If so, the student is communicating and succeeding.

After the entire presentation, I ask the student, who is still in front of the class, to talk about the interview and the question and answer process. What did the student find helpful and/or difficult? In addition to the reflection paper, this gives students an opportunity to reflect on the enactment they have just experienced.

WRITING AND ENACTING MONOLOGUES

Students sign up to write a monologue for either Sarah or Hagar from Genesis (see number 3 in Presentations Sign-up List). A monologue is written in the first person. It gives a student an opportunity to identify with a character (encourage male students to do this exercise–to find the Hagar or Sarah in themselves). At the same time, students read midrash and exegetical readings of the Abrahamic cycle. They choose a part of the story they will interpret. The monologue must also express the point of view of at least one of the authors read. The students write and memorize their monologues. Just as with the interviews, the presenting student improvises answers to questions from other students following the monologue. These enactments, oral and written, blend personal insights into Sarah and Hagar with scholarly perspectives.

EVALUATING MONOLOGUES

- Does the monologue communicate a character with a point of view? Is that point of view inclusive of an author from the class readings? Has the student added her own perspective?
- Does the monologue take place in a specific time and place (see chapter 4)?
- Has the student memorized the written text (rather than improvised a quasi-rendition/facsimile of it)?

  Note: ask the student for a copy of the monologue before the enactment; ask another student to follow the text of the written monologue during the enactment. This student can offer forgotten lines and/or can be asked afterward how well the student did in sticking to the text. It's also advisable for you to receive a copy of the monologue afterward.

- The audience/class is an integral part of this work. Is the student speaking clearly for all to hear? (If the student is rushing her words, ask her to speak more slowly, and breathe!)
- Does the student communicate the character—in voice, language, gesture, body?
- Does the student show the integration of his point of view with that of the readings during the improvisatory question and answer period?

  Note: I give students a chance to enact the memorized monologue a second time. It often allows understandable nervousness to melt away, so the character can be better revealed.

MEMORIZATION AND ENACTMENT OF SACRED TEXTS

Certainly memorizing a text does not mean that a student understands it. Understanding occurs on a continuum, meaning it is part of a process of knowing. Thus memorization of a text is combined with verbal and written reflection as well as testing and the final paper of the course. In the memorization of texts such as the Qur'an, the Upanishads, Thich Nhat Hanh's gathas, the Bhagavad Gita, and Rumi, assessment is based on how well a student has internalized the words of a text (chapter 5). "How well" may appear to be a "fuzzy" term, but when you hear a text spoken, you know right away if it is wooden and devoid of meaning or if the speaker has infused it with understanding. Another way to observe meaning using external methods is almost painterly, to notice the clarity of the words, their shading in terms of texture, color, rhythm. "How well" also refers to the ability of the student to articulate his/her experience and understanding of the text in the discussion period following the enacted text.

EVALUATING MEMORIZATION AND ENACTMENT OF SACRED TEXTS

- Do the words of the text, when they are heard by you, feel as if their meaning is understood?
- Are the words of the text spoken clearly and accurately?

  Note: each time a student offers a memorized piece, it helps to give another student a copy of it to follow along if lines are forgotten by the presenter.
- The audience/class is an integral part of this work. Is the student speaking clearly for all to hear? (If the student is rushing her words, ask her to speak more slowly, and breathe!)
- Are the words of the text given texture, coloring, rhythm?

  Note: Mechanical speaking of the words shows either terror or a lack of understanding of the text and its relationship to the speaker. Have a student recite a text twice, since the first time is usually full of nervousness. The second time the words are usually filled with more feeling. Again, I am not looking for "acting" but instead a commitment to giving voice to the words and their meaning.
- In the discussion afterward, ask the student to reflect on the meaning of the words memorized. Did the process of memorization help to reveal the meaning of the text? How do the words of the text affect you? *Note:* some of this response will no doubt be mirrored in the student's reflection paper.

FINAL PAPER: SCENE AND ANALYSIS

As a final paper, students write a dramatic scene. They combine research, class readings, and lectures with their imagination. I have used this method in different ways over the years. In my biblical drama classes, each student rewrites a biblical story as a contemporary scene. In a course called Millennial Thinking, each student interviewed five to six people asking what the year 2000 meant to them, and then wove the interviews into a one-act play. In a course entitled

Toxic Avengers Theatre, which explored environmental hazards, students interned in groups of two with selected community organizations; they researched an issue addressed by the organization. As a team, the two students wrote a full-length play about an environmental issue using the experience of their internship, class readings, research, and required footnotes.

In Intro to Religious Studies, I ask students to write a fifteen-page paper: five pages a dramatic dialogue, followed by analysis of the topic explored. Scene writing evaluates how students apply their knowledge of religions and research skills in a creative manner. I include the specific assignment here:

Final Assignment: Write a Scene and Analysis

- Write a five-page dialogue between two characters of different religions regarding an ethical issue. (e.g., sin, intermarriage, abortion, environment, death).

  Note: Regarding using sources in your plays—I'm interested in having you put into your own words and the words of your characters the readings and research that each of you has done in this course. I'm NOT interested in characters that simply spout out words from a book or who are speaking in direct quotes from a book. I AM interested in how you understand what you have read—through what your characters say. This will show me how you integrate the ideas of the readings, your research, and your imagination.

  As part of the dialogue, when a character speaks any thought that references class readings or your independent research, you should reference its source by using footnotes/endnotes, or works cited.

- Provide a specific place, time, character descriptions, and staging notes.
- Ten pages of your paper will be an analysis of the ethical issue and its explication in the scene.

- Bibliography required.
- Due the last day of the class.

A Note of Caution to Teachers

I hope that you will not use the scene writing technique described above without using other theatre techniques suggested in this book. It is important that students be acquainted with developing characters (through sculpting, improvisations, enactments, and play reading) before they write scenes. From play reading, improvisations, and character monologues, they have experienced what good dialogue is. Thus students are prepared by the end of the semester to write these scenes.

Hand Out: Tips for Writing Scenes

1. Listen to conversations to hear how people talk.
2. Get rid of the judge on your shoulder—tell him[or her] to come back some other time.
3. Start with the two characters you want to work with. Imagine them: how they are dressed, how they walk. In your mind's eye, let them introduce themselves to you. As you listen to them, watch them to see what their behavior is like.
4. A scene begins, has a middle, and has an end. The action and dialogue of the scene can already be in progress when the scene starts. Or the beginning can really be the beginning.
5. A scene has a specific place and time (e.g., a cold winter night; the house is silent except for the crackling of a bright fire; the time is midnight). Take the time to see it carefully in your mind's eye and describe it for the reader before the dialogue begins.
6. Before the dialogue begins, name and describe each character.
7. Show, don't tell. Try not to say directly in words what you can convey indirectly through behavior. And never sermonize.

8. It's good to leave some elements unresolved.
9. Avoid telling the audience what to feel. Let the characters say what they want.
10. Each character in your scene speaks in a different way (word choices, expressions).
11. Use silence.
12. Try not to create a "pat," "sugar-coated" ending. Not all stories end nicely.[1]

An example of a student paper in my Intro to Religious Studies course was a scene between two people contemplating marriage, a Jewish man and a Catholic woman. His family is a mixture of cultural Jews and those from the Reformist tradition. Her family is conservative Roman Catholic. Both the man and woman practice their faiths. The moral dilemma explored in the scene was, in which faith do we raise the children? The dialogue is set inside a car parked at the ocean, on a late spring evening following a dinner with his family. The dialogue reveals that he previously had agreed to have their children raised Catholic. However, just an hour ago at dinner with his family, he began to see the importance of passing on his own religious tradition to his children. In the course of the dialogue in the car, the man and woman ponder the positions of their traditions about inter-marriage. The scene ends with the couple questioning whether their love can carry them over the resistance of their families and the traditions of their religions. The student footnoted his sources during the dialogue and followed it with ten pages that analyzed Jewish and Catholic positions on intermarriage and the dilemma of his characters.

In my biblical drama course, three biblical stories are studied during the semester. The culmination of each story is a student's contemporary interpretation of the biblical story that uses research and class readings. One recent student put it this way:

> I, as writer, was God in this instance. With the power of my pen I had the ability to rewrite or interject a detail that softened the Biblical account much the way Sleeping Beauty's fairy godmother modified the witch's cruel death curse to a sleeping spell that could be broken with a kiss. I filled in those moments the Biblical writer left unaccounted and supposed a scenario that changed everything I was made to feel about Sarai, Abram, and Hagar. In so doing, I uncovered things about myself and stretched a hand across the centuries that began to reclaim these characters as missing pieces of myself.[2]

As with all other assessment activities, students must know how they will be assessed, what you are looking for, and what standards are expected. When I began teaching some twenty years ago, I thought that evaluation was a process that only I engaged in, as if I was sitting in a dark theatre like a director evaluating the performance of actors. Through the guidance of my peers, I began to see how powerfully students meet goals when they know them. When a student knows that the class wants him to succeed, that we eagerly await the words of the Gita or Thich Nhat Hanh from him, there is a need to fulfill our hopes as he shapes and gives voice to the words. When a student knows that we are eager to see her transform and become a character with her voice, body, and gestures (however she is able to do this), she will strain with her whole being to give this to us. Yes, there is always hesitancy at the beginning of doing something new. But gradually this is overcome. When a memorized piece is said a second time by a student, her spirit heaves a sigh of relief that she has accomplished the piece once and now the ground feels firmer and she can literally inhabit the words.

Part of evaluation is also understanding an individual student's needs. There may be students who might find enactment extremely stressful and for whom you will need to help or modify the situation. It is a fine line to distinguish between challenging/supporting a student to push past fears and seeing that an enactment might be causing too much pressure or stress. Though I have not had this occur in my own experience, it could happen. And if it does, perhaps creating one-on-one sessions between you and the student for enactment may be helpful. From this base of trust, the student's confidence and strength can be built.

This chapter and its focus on assessment is but a draft of ideas for you. As you venture into using enactment more frequently in your courses, you will bring your own clarity and approach to this process. And I hope that you will share them with me!

8

the comfort-fear spectrum

WHEN I BEGAN TEACHING, I was nervous. In doing M.Div. and Ph.D. studies, I'd spent a lot of time watching great professors. Course readings, discussions, and papers occupied most of my university life. In that learning process, I never took a course or was required to take a course on pedagogy. There was little talk of pedagogy. So when I began teaching, I was filled with anxiety and fear. Can I teach? Can I engage in dialogue with my students? Can I lecture? What if I don't know enough? I wonder if you are chuckling because you recognize these feelings. But like anything else, like lecturing for the first time, I got used to it by doing it, by experiencing it, by repetition. I found techniques that fit my teaching styles through trial and error. I found what works for me and for my students.

I suggest that, in the beginning, you will want to choose in which course or courses to try these techniques. Pick and choose from this book exercises that you want to try (and make up your own as well!). And as I have urged repeatedly, on the first day of class, introduce students to at least one theatre exercise so that they will know to expect this method throughout the semester.

Recently, I asked a colleague who uses my theatre methods in her religious studies courses to tell me how she approached her own fear when she began.

> I wasn't enjoying teaching. All I knew was the traditional model of lecturing. I was looking to make it more fun and creative for myself. I'd been teaching ten years. I needed to be more engaged. . . . At first, in using theatre, I was nervous. I didn't want to project that to the class. I mean, I'd never experienced this kind of work as a teacher or a student. I was uncomfortable asking people to do what I'd never done. But through trying things, I began to get used to it and found how powerful this work can be, for me and for my students.

When we try something new, like the method of using theatre, we come up against our fears of the other. Perhaps the question is how to meet this "other" as a friend, for you the teacher and your students. Like any relationship, a friendship takes time to know the other. My colleague continued:

> I'm a person who likes to test the waters and not be thrown in. I like to take it slow. I become more comfortable through experience. So I tried small things in the beginning that were less threatening, so I could build on that. Once the group felt comfortable as a group, they were more willing to take risks. As their comfort level increased, so did mine. Some students volunteer right away and then others follow suit. A student said to me, there's no way I'm acting! By the end of the semester she was acting and enjoying it.

I agree with my colleague that the vast majority of students enter into theatre exercises and enjoy them. It is also important to add that students' fears in participating or enacting theatre can be for different reasons. It is impossible to intuit those reasons. Bodies hold memories. This is why, particularly in the beginning of the semester, I outline an exercise before doing it with a class. I make it clear that it is up to each student to know her parameters, his needs, her history. If the student doesn't want to do the exercise, I respect that. I try to find a way to talk with that student about it at another time, one on one. Often such a student sees in later exercises that she can choose how much of herself she wants to invest, Theatre is not losing control, but instead a delicate balance between control of the body and emotions and simultaneously a surrender of that which we wish to reveal about ourselves. Seeing the safety of exercises and the enjoyment had by most, this student will gradually enter into the flow.

As teachers, sometimes doubting voices creep into our interior landscapes. That's what fear does. What allows us to get past fears? Students. It is clear that students appreciate a new approach. They are energized by it. Student interest creates a vibrant learning environment. Students enjoy learning using theatre. Listen to the students:

- I have learned the importance for me of getting out of my head and of speaking to and with my body. I found the channel of communication in the bodily form—clear, swift, and forceful.
- This course challenged me to think in ways that I normally would not, in a religious standpoint. I was able to use movement to describe how I think and feel.
- I definitely learned a lot about religion I never knew before. Not just knowing the words or ideas, but feeling what it means to understand them, and to know what effect this understanding could have on my life.
- Dr. Rue makes us do things physically. For example, act in front of the class, which I believe is a great technique to learn with.
- I have improved my ability to be more open to others' points of view.

I include student comments here, made at the end of the semester, to remind myself, and perhaps you, that this is not where they start. Students begin by reading in your course description that theatre will be used as a methodology. Thus they arrive expecting it. Even with that expectation, students will be shy, hesitant, and in need of your encouragement. Your encouragement, coupled with their energetic and positive responses, will in turn offer you the courage to go forward. And when you are consistent with the use of theatre methods in your classroom sessions, comments like the preceding ones will describe the results for your students.

Theatre is movement, feeling, and thought. Perhaps the thinking part of this statement is not the stumbling block for you. But introducing students to movement and encountering their feelings while engaging in critical thinking—that perhaps is something new. When a student experiences an emotion such as peace while doing the action and text of a gatha by Thich Nhat Hanh, the student has discovered through his own internal life the truth of the words. No lecture or Power Point presentation can provide this. This is bodied knowledge. As I said in chapter 5, this approach will ask students to encounter themselves, perhaps in a new way. Perhaps new feelings will emerge. Students can experience not only a new idea, but also a visceral understanding of the Divine through speaking aloud a memorized scripture fragment. As a teacher I celebrate this as a successful moment. If students discover a positive feeling for a religion, or at least a new openness toward a faith, this is also a success. Given the state of our warring world, it is incumbent upon us as teachers to open doors of understanding and empathy towards religions, doors of new ideas and yes, feelings, to unblock fear and prejudice.

Perhaps some will criticize the use of theatre in the religious studies or theology classroom as being akin to an encounter group, psychodrama, or group therapy, or a veiled attempt at getting students to talk about their traumatic experiences. Not so, dear reader. Those systems are focused on the problems of individuals and have much benefit. But what I am presenting in this book is the use of theatre to illuminate and embody religious experience. Certainly in so doing we are building bridges between ourselves and individuals who live and breathe in other faiths and cultures. Certainly in so doing we may discover new insights, emotions, sensations about our own life journeys. But the goal is to open empathy and understanding of the other and the other's faith experience through the thought, movement, and feeling of the theatre.

You may ask, by implication, what is the place of emotion in the classroom? It is my firm belief that learning is an emotional act. Learning with the body must include our emotions. bell hooks says that some of her colleagues walking by a classroom where students are engaged in working, in tears, or amidst smiling and laughter, make an assumption:

> If it's emotional, it's a kind of group therapy. Few professors talk about the place of emotions in the classroom. . . . When we bring our passion to the classroom our collective passions come together, and there is often an emotional response, one that can overwhelm. . . . Whenever emotional responses erupt, many of us believe our academic purpose has been diminished. If we focus on not just whether emotions produce pleasure or pain, but on how they keep us alert, we are reminded that they enhance classrooms.[1]

Feelings also assist students to understand what they've been reading. Critical thinking and enactment create emotional learning. This is what is needed in the classroom. Emotions are engagement. They are internal experience. The study of religion is the study of emotional material. How can we teach religion without emotions? How can we expect students to find their internal truths without engaging their internal experience, which is emotion? The exercises in this book offer forms that have clear beginnings and endings. Each one is a frame into which students can safely place their emotions. These exercises of the theatre invite teachers and students into mapped areas that in traditional lecturing are avoided: emotional control, the place and importance of emotion in the educational enterprise, and opportunities to create language with which to express emotion.

Teachers, in understanding the import of internal experience, must also be able to hold, handle, and embrace what they are asking students to do. If teachers are not prepared for students to cry, or be angry, sad, or uncomfortable, then students feel they did something wrong in expressing such feelings. They regret it or feel embarrassed. But if the teacher embraces feeling as a way of knowing, the student sees it's okay. Again, I asked my colleague about her experience in teaching with emotions.

> It's when students don't have feelings that I mind. In my course, Women and Religion, if students aren't working on a feeling level, there's something wrong. These theater techniques help students to connect with their emotions and better understand the reading.

As teachers, we wish to work with those younger than ourselves to inspire, co-create, and dialogue about new knowledge. But often we fear the other. Perhaps we feel that the other will destabilize our own sense of who we think we are. I am reminded of Parker Palmer's clarification, "Be not afraid." He suggests that the phrase does not mean that we will not have fears. Instead, he says, we needn't *be* our fears.[2] "Be not afraid" means that we can choose not to act or teach out of fear. So if fear of trying a new method such as theatre exists in you, be not afraid, you are not that fear. You are something larger. And sometimes, we find out who we are through witnessing the beauty and wholeness of our students as they step into a theatre exercise that we have invited them to do.

conclusion

> In our present state of degeneration, it is through the skin that metaphysics must be made to reenter our minds.[1]

THIS BOOK AT ITS ROOT ARGUES FOR UNDERSTANDING religions and faiths as housed in the body and experienced through action/embodiment. Theatre incarnates. It is the handmaiden of experiencing religion. Theatre in the religious studies or theology classroom plunges the student and teacher into methods that result in momentary immersions into particular religions.

Core to this pedagogy is a focus on religious experience. With my work, I invite students to swim into the waters of bodied knowledge—for a moment to feel the depth, expanse, and particularity of a religion. For a moment to meet an idea and try it on. For a moment to act as if he or she believed. This is the position of bodied knowledge, which champions the body, lived experience, relationship/mutuality, and community as ways of knowing.

In religious studies, theatre as pedagogy becomes a divining rod that points to sacred waters and offers students moments of particular enacted experience in each religion. In theology, theatre befriends faith. From this meeting, faith is experienced as housed in the body and experienced through action/embodiment. Yet for both religious studies and theology, this pedagogy demands the unlocking of hermetically sealed positions that idolize on the one hand the impossible view of an objective/neutral approach to religion and on the other a pristine belief that is untouched by its social/political context. Instead, bringing theatre into the classroom will be disruptive, questioning, shifting, complex.

Provocative and messy, like life, theatre situates religions and faiths into contexts with faces. Challenging and unsettling, theatre inspires creative interpretations and points of view that one day may lead to new visions. And for me, this is exactly the breath of new life that is needed.

What are the results of using theatre as pedagogy? Students understand religion(s) from an interior and exterior perspective. Students invest corporeality in learning. Students walk away from a semester's course having met themselves and their peers on the journey. Students try out or rehearse in the classroom visions, thoughts, and beliefs that they may choose to enact in their everyday lives. They have gained a religious sensibility, thought fleshed out through enactment. And what of teachers, you may ask? Teachers using theatre in religious studies and theology discover holistic learning as they combine the cognitive with the experiential. Reaching into the sphere of enacted knowledge, instructors witness the depth of the human spirit through the creativity of their students and themselves.

Beyond the classroom, this book is a clarion call to experience the inherent value of each religion in our world. I write to urge teachers to teach religion focused on religious experience—experience that can be communicated through theatre, a medium that is all about embodied experience and empathy. Religion is powerful. We see that, finally, in the tragic events of our time that pit religion against religion. Courageous teachers and questioning students can move us past these barriers of ideology into the heart—not to exclude the head—but to remember the heart, for that is where we all meet. Not Jew or Greek, female or male, gay or straight . . . but in the experience of the heart, we are sisters and brothers of the Divine. We are what we receive, said a priest at Mass the other day. Yes, we are what God is, said the Beguines of the Middle Ages (who were later burned for it). That is the place of the heart. This is my goal, through theatre and religion, to enter the place of the heart, to realize, appreciate, distinguish the beauty of different religions and how we meet in the heart of the universe.

What remains important—no matter the form or space—is that embodied and enacted creativity be brought to the realm of religious studies and theology. As we stand at the beginning of the twenty-first century, the search for meaning becomes more visceral. Whether it is hip-hop or in-your-face behavior, cross dressing or virtual reality, we are reviewing our human situation. The old forms of religion are both revived and falling away. Meaning is being both channeled and defrauded. Spiritualities are both abundant and sometimes vacuous. Into this miasma, the concreteness of everyday life as the site of the Holy is reassuring and clarifying. In our classrooms, theatre enacting theologies and religions can create visions of everyday sacrality that challenge and expand the future for ourselves and our globe. Our classrooms can illuminate the body-soul journey of women and men working for a just world where the work of the Sacred is seen as truly our own.

notes

Introduction

1. Victoria Rue, "Feminist Theatre Enacts Feminist Theology in the Play *CancerBodies:* Women Speaking the Unspeakable," (dissertation, the Graduate Theological Union, Berkeley, 1993).

Chapter One

1. Gerardus Van Der Leeuw, *Sacred and Profane Beauty: The Holy in Art,* trans. David E. Gree (New York: Holt, Rinehart and Winston, 1963).

2. Otilio Rodriguez and Kiernan Kavanaugh, trans., *Teresa of Avila, Meditations on the Song of Songs, Vol. II: The Collected Works of St. Teresa of Avila* (Washington D.C.: Carmelites Studies. 1980), 234.

3. Emilie Zum Brunn and Georgette Epiney Burgard, *Women Mystics in Medieval Europe* (New York: Paragon House, 1989), 47.

4. Beverly W. Harrison. *Our Right to Choose: Toward a New Ethic of Abortion* (Boston: Beacon Press, 1983), 106, 108.

5. Hyun Kyung Chung, *Struggle to Be the Sun Again: Introducing Asian Women's Theology* (Maryknoll, N.Y.: Orbis Books, 1990), 104.

6. Helen Keller, *The Story of My Life* (Garden City: Doubleday, 1921), 23–24. Copyright © 1904 Helen Keller. With permission of the American Foundation for the Blind.

7. bell hooks, *Teaching to Transgress: Education as the Practice of Freedom* (New York: Routledge, 1994), 137.

8. Emily Shihadeh and Victoria Rue, *Grapes and Figs Are in Season: A Palestinian Woman's Story* (unpublished play script, 1991).

9. Elizabeth Dodson Gray, ed., *Sacred Dimensions of Women's Experience* (Wellesley, Mass.: Roundtable Press, 1988).

10. Parker J. Palmer, *The Courage to Teach: Exploring the Inner Landscape of a Teacher's Life* (San Francisco: Jossey-Bass, 1998), 12.

11. Carter Heyward, *God in the Balance: Christian Spirituality in Times of Terror* (Cleveland: Pilgrim Press, 2002), 74, 75.

12. Thich Nhat Hanh, *Being Peace* (Berkeley: Parallax Press, 1987), 68.

13. hooks, *Teaching to Transgress,* 138.

Chapter Two

1. Good websites that offer views of the exercise: www.hathayogalesson.com/sunsal.html; www.personal.psu.edu/faculty/j/c/jcw23/salut.html

2. Kristin Linklater, *Freeing the Natural Voice* (New York: Drama Publishers, 1976), 1–2.

3. Paul Dennison and Gail E. Dennison, *Brain Gym,* teacher's edition revised (Ventura: Edu-Kinesthetics, 1989) 30.

4. A resource for this work is Nelle Morton's *The Journey Is Home* (Boston: Beacon Press, 1986), especially her well-known phrase "hearing someone into speech." The phrase refers to being with another who is unable to speak his or her thoughts/feelings, waiting respectfully, offering space until the words are found.

5. Fran Grace, e-mail correspondence with author, November 2, 2002.

6. With an internet search engine, type in the key words "theater exercises" and you will encounter countless books on the subject. My favorites are works by Keith Johnstone, Augusto Boal, Viola Spolin, and the Open Theater.

Chapter Three

1. Lynda Sexson,. *Ordinarily Sacred* (Charlottesville: University Press of Virginia, 1992), 55.

2. Judith Plaskow, *Standing Again at Sinai: Judaism from a Feminist Perspective.* (San Francisco: HarperSanFrancisco, 1991); Abraham Heschel, *Between God and Man: An Interpretation of Judaism* (New York: Free Press Paperbacks, 1997).

3. Leonard Bernstein, "Kaddish," in *Judaica,* compact disc (Hamburg: Universal Music Group, Deutsche Grammophone, GmbH, 1999).

4. Augusto Boal, *Theatre of the Oppressed* (New York: Urizen Books, 1979).

5. Victoria Rue, "Putting Flesh on the Bones of God," *SEMEIA : Biblical Glamour and Hollywood Glitz,* 74 (1997): 189.

6. Gary David Comstock, *Violence Against Lesbians and Gay Men* (New York: Columbia University Press, 1991), 128–40.

7. Coleman Barks, *Rumi: We Are Three: New Rumi Poems* (Athens, Ga.: Maypop Books, 1988).

8. Frithjof Schuon, *Understanding Islam* (Bloomington, Ind.: World Wisdom Books, 1998).

9. Ahmed, Akbar S., *Islam Today: A Short Introduction to the Muslim World* (London: I.B. Tauris, 2002).

Chapter Four

1. Viola Spolin, *Improvisation for the Theatre: A Handbook of Teaching and Directing Techniques,* 3d ed. (Evanston, Ill.: Northwestern University Press, 1999), 4.

2. Ibid., 6.

3. Sonia Moore, *Training the Actor: The Stanislavski System in Class* (New York: Penguin Books, 1979), 46.

4. Spolin, *Improvisation,* 253. Chapter 12 in Spolin is devoted to other "Who am I?" exercises.

5. Spolin, *Improvisation,* 89. Chapter 4 in Spolin is devoted to "Where?" exercises.

6. Adriene Thorne, "Overturned Text Brings Understanding, Healing, and Release–Aligning Mind, Body and Spirit" (student paper, excerpted with permission, Graduate Theological Union, Berkeley, June 2004).

7. Jonathan Evans. "Insights" (student paper, excerpted with permission, Graduate Theological Union, Berkeley, June 2004).

Chapter Five

1. Robert E. Van Voorst, *Anthology of World Scriptures* (Toronto: Wadsworth/Thomson Learning, 2003), 285.

2. Gary E. Kessler, comp., *Ways of Being Religious,* "Bhagavad-Gita," trans. Barbara Stoler Miller (Mountain View, Calif.: Mayfield Publishing, 2000) 135, 136.

3. Reprinted from Thich Nhat Hanh, *Present Moment, Wonderful Moment* (Berkeley, Parallax Press. 1990), 48, with permission of Parallax Press, www.parallax.org.

4. Ibid., 11.

5. Ibid., 14.

6. Ibid., 13.

7. D.O. Lyon, *Memory and the Learning Process* (Baltimore: Warwick and York, 1917), 13.

8. Paul E. and Gail E. Dennison, *Brain Gym, Teachers Edition* (Ventura: Edu-Kinesthetics, 1994), 30.

9. Hanh, *Present Moment,* 32.

10. Carol Lloyd, "Voice of America," Salon/Brilliant Careers, December 1998, http://www.salon.com/bc/1998/12/cov_08bc.html.

11. Ibid. Other books by Anna Deavere Smith: *Fires in the Mirror: Crown Heights, Brooklyn, and Other Identities* (New York: Anchor

Paperback, 1993) and *Talk to Me: Travels in Media and Politics* (New York: Anchor/Doubleday, 2001).

Chaper Six

1. Peter Brook, *The Empty Space* (New York: Atheneum, 1982).
2. Antonin Artaud, *The Theatre and its Double,* trans. Mary Caroline Richards (New York: Grove Press, 1958).
3. Gerardus Van Der Leeuw, *Sacred and Profane Beauty: The Holy in Art,* trans. David E. Green (New York: Holt, Rinehart and Winston, 1963).
4. Max Harris, *The Theatre and Incarnation* (New York: St.Martin's Press, 1990), 2.
5. Friedrich Heer, *The Medieval World* (New York: Mentor Books, 1961).
6. V. A. Kolve, *The Play Called Corpus Christi.* (Stanford: Stanford University Press, 1966), 7.
7. Lenora Inez Brown, "Writing Religion: Is God a Character in Your Plays?" *American Theatre Magazine* (November 2000), 30.
8. Jane Martin, *Talking With* (New York: Samuel French, 1983), 37.
9. Ibid., 40.
10. Ibid., 49.
11. Letitia Bartlett and Victoria Rue, *Ecstasy in the Everyday* (unpublished manuscript, 1992).
12. Ahmed Ibrahim Al-Fagih, "The Singing of the Stars," from *Short Arabic Plays: An Anthology,* ed. Salma Khadra Jayyusi, published by Interlink Books, an imprint of Interlink Publishing Group, Inc; www.interlinkbooks.com. Text copyright ©Salma Khadra Jayyusi, 2003. Reprinted by permission.
13. Ibid.
14. Tony Kushner, *Angels in America: A Gay Fantasia on American Themes,* "Part One: Millennium Approaches," scene 7, act 2 (New York: Theatre Communications Group, 1992), 74.
15. Caryl Churchill, *Vinegar Tom, in Plays: One: Owners, Traps, Vinegar Tom, Light Shining* in *Buckinghamshire, Cloud Nine* (London and New York: Methuen Publishing Ltd., and Routledge, 1985).

16. Victoria Rue, "The Landscape of My Body" (master's thesis, Union Theological Seminary, 1988).

17. Sandy Butler and Barbara Rosenblum, *Cancer in Two Voices,* 2d ed. (Denver: Spinsters Ink Books, 1996).

18. Victoria Rue, "Feminist Theatre Enacts Feminist Theology in the Play *CancerBodies: Women Speaking the Unspeakable* (doctoral dissertation, Graduate Theological Union, 1993).

19. Merle Feld, "Across the Jordan," in *Making a Scene: the Contemporary Drama of Jewish-American Women,* ed. Sarah Blacher Cohen (Syracuse: Syracuse University Press, 1997), 329.

20. Kahlil Gibran, *Jesus the Son of Man: His Words and His Deeds as Told and Recorded by Those Who Knew Him* (New York: Alfred A Knopf, 1970), 68.

21. Ehn, Erik, *The Saint Plays* (New York: Performing Arts Journal Books, 2000).

22. CeliaWren, "Saints, Sin, and Erik Ehn: Mysticism Ignites the Plays—and Theories—of a Theatrical Visionary," *American Theatre Magazine* (May/June 2004), 21, 22.

23. Swami Prabhavananda and Christopher Isherwood, trans., *The Song of God: Bhagavad-Gita* (New York: Mentor Books, 1972), 57.

24. Jean-Claude Carriere and Peter Brook, *The Mahabharata, a Play Based upon the Indian Classic Epic* (New York: Harper & Row, 1985), ix.

25. Thich Nhat Hanh, *Love in Action: Writings on Nonviolent Social Change.* (Berkeley, California: Parallax Press, 1993), 73.

26. Thich Nhat Hanh, *Love in Action,* 9.

27. Ibid., 12.

28. Ibid., 6.

29. Salah 'Abd al-Sabur. Khalil I. Semaan, trans. *Murder in Baghdad* (Ma'sat al-Hallaj) (Leiden: E. J. Brill, 1972), also (Cairo: General Egyptian Book Organization, 1976).

30. www.cornerstone.org.

31. www.atjt.com.

Chapter Seven

1. Adapted from David Copelin, *Practical Playwriting* (Boston: Writer, 1998), 7–12.

2. Adriene Thorne, "Overturned Text Brings Understanding, Healing, and Release—Aligning Mind, Body and Spirit" (student paper, excerpted with permission, Graduate Theological Union, Berkeley June, 2004.

Chapter Eight

1. bell hooks, *Teaching to Transgress: Education as the Practice of Freedom* (New York: Routledge, 1994), 154, 155.

2. Parker Palmer. *The Courage to Teach: Exploring the Inner Landscape of a Teacher's Life* (San Francisco: Jossey-Bass, 1998), 57.

Conclusion

1. Antonin Artaud, *The Theatre and Its Double* (New York: Grove Press, 1958).

Related Titles from The Pilgrim Press

PROVOKING THE GOSPEL
Methods to Embody Biblical Storytelling through Drama

Richard W. Swanson

This unique "how-to" and "why-to" resource shows those in ministry or preparing for a religious vocation how to embody the gospel through the techniques of drama and storytelling.

ISBN 0-8298-1573-2
Paper, 160 pages
$18.00

PROVOKING THE GOSPEL OF MARK
A Storyteller's Commentary, Year B

Richard W. Swanson

The first book—Year B—in a new series that shows how to provoke fresh understandings of the gospel texts and embody them through drama and storytelling.

ISBN 0-8298-1690-9
Paper over board—with DVD, 352 pages
$35.00

To order these or any other books from The Pilgrim Press, call or write to:

The Pilgrim Press
700 Prospect Avenue
Cleveland, OH 44115-1100

Phone orders: 800-537-3394 (M–F, 8:30am–4:30pm ET)
Fax orders: 216-736-2206

Please include shipping charges of $5.00 for the first book and 75¢ for each additional book.

Or order from our web site at www.thepilgrimpress.com.

Prices subject to change without notice.